T0256263

# Teaching Cybersecurity

Let's be realistic here. Ordinary K-12 educators don't know what "cybersecurity" is and could probably care less about incorporating it into their lesson plans. Yet, teaching cybersecurity is a critical national priority. So, this book aims to cut through the usual roadblocks of confusing technical jargon and industry stovepipes and give you, the classroom teacher, a unified understanding of what must be taught. That advice is based on a single authoritative definition of the field. In 2017, the three societies that write the standards for computing, software engineering, and information systems came together to define a single model of the field of cybersecurity. It is based on eight building blocks. That definition is presented here. However, we also understand that secondary school teachers are not experts in arcane subjects like software, component, human, or societal security. Therefore, this book explains cybersecurity through a simple story rather than diving into execution details. Tom, a high school teacher, and Lucy, a middle school teacher, are tasked by their district to develop a cybersecurity course for students in their respective schools. They are aided in this by "the Doc," an odd fellow but an expert in the field. Together they work their way through the content of each topic area, helping each other to understand what the student at each level in the educational process has to learn. The explanations are simple, easy to understand, and geared toward the teaching aspect rather than the actual performance of cybersecurity work. Each chapter is a self-contained explanation of the cybersecurity content in that area geared to teaching both middle and high school audiences. The eight component areas are standalone in that they can be taught separately. But the real value lies in the comprehensive but easy-to-understand picture that the reader will get of a complicated field.

## Security, Audit and Leadership Series

*Series Editor: Dan Swanson, Dan Swanson and Associates, Ltd., Winnipeg, Manitoba, Canada.*

The Security, Audit and Leadership Series publishes leading-edge books on critical subjects facing security and audit executives as well as business leaders. Key topics addressed include Leadership, Cybersecurity, Security Leadership, Privacy, Strategic Risk Management, Auditing IT, Audit Management and Leadership

*Agile Enterprise Risk Management: Risk-Based Thinking, Multi-Disciplinary Management and Digital Transformation*
Howard M. Wiener

*Information System Audit: How to Control the Digital Disruption*
Philippe Peret

*Agile Audit Transformation and Beyond*
Toby DeRoche

*Mind the Tech Gap: Addressing the Conflicts between IT and Security Teams*
Nikki Robinson

*CyRM$^{SM}$: Mastering the Management of Cybersecurity*
David X Martin

*The Auditor's Guide to Blockchain Technology: Architecture, Use Cases, Security and Assurance*
Shaun Aghili

*Artificial Intelligence Perspective for Smart Cities*
Vahap Tecim and Sezer Bozkus Kahyaoglu

*Teaching Cybersecurity: A Handbook for Teaching the Cybersecurity Body of Knowledge in a Conventional Classroom*
Daniel Shoemaker, Ken Sigler and Tamara Shoemaker

*Cognitive Risk*
James Bone and Jessie H Lee

*Privacy in Practice: Establish and Operationalize a Holistic Data Privacy Program*
Alan Tang

For more information about this series, please visit: https://www.routledge.com/Internal-Audit-and-IT-Audit/book-series/CRCINTAUDITA

# Teaching Cybersecurity
## A Handbook for Teaching
## the Cybersecurity Body of Knowledge
## in a Conventional Classroom

Daniel Shoemaker, Ken Sigler, and
Tamara Shoemaker

CRC Press
Taylor & Francis Group
Boca Raton  London  New York

CRC Press is an imprint of the
Taylor & Francis Group, an **informa** business

First edition published 2023
by CRC Press
6000 Broken Sound Parkway NW, Suite 300, Boca Raton, FL 33487-2742

and by CRC Press
4 Park Square, Milton Park, Abingdon, Oxon, OX14 4RN

*CRC Press is an imprint of Taylor & Francis Group, LLC*

© 2023 Daniel Shoemaker, Ken Sigler and Tamara Shoemaker

Reasonable efforts have been made to publish reliable data and information, but the author and publisher cannot assume responsibility for the validity of all materials or the consequences of their use. The authors and publishers have attempted to trace the copyright holders of all material reproduced in this publication and apologize to copyright holders if permission to publish in this form has not been obtained. If any copyright material has not been acknowledged please write and let us know so we may rectify in any future reprint.

Except as permitted under U.S. Copyright Law, no part of this book may be reprinted, reproduced, transmitted, or utilized in any form by any electronic, mechanical, or other means, now known or hereafter invented, including photocopying, microfilming, and recording, or in any information storage or retrieval system, without written permission from the publishers.

For permission to photocopy or use material electronically from this work, access www.copyright.com or contact the Copyright Clearance Center, Inc. (CCC), 222 Rosewood Drive, Danvers, MA 01923, 978-750-8400. For works that are not available on CCC please contact mpkbookspermissions@tandf.co.uk

*Trademark notice*: Product or corporate names may be trademarks or registered trademarks and are used only for identification and explanation without intent to infringe.

---

**Library of Congress Cataloging-in-Publication Data**

---

Names: Shoemaker, Dan, author. | Sigler, Kenneth, author. | Shoemaker, Tamara, (Cyber security expert), author.
Title: Teaching cybersecurity : a handbook for teaching the cybersecurity body of knowledge in a conventional classroom / Daniel Shoemaker, Ken Sigler, and Tamara Shoemaker.
Description: First edition. | Boca Raton, FL : CRC Press, 2023. | Series: Security, Audit and Leadership Series | Includes bibliographical references.
Identifiers: LCCN 2022038672 (print) | LCCN 2022038673 (ebook) | ISBN 9781032034089 (hbk) | ISBN 9781032034096 (pbk) | ISBN 9781003187172 (ebk)
Subjects: LCSH: Computer networks--Security measures--Study and teaching. | Internet--Security measures--Study and teaching.
Classification: LCC TK5105.59 S56 2023 (print) | LCC TK5105.59 (ebook) | DDC 005.8071--dc23/eng/20221018
LC record available at https://lccn.loc.gov/2022038672
LC ebook record available at https://lccn.loc.gov/2022038673

---

ISBN: 978-1-032-03408-9 (hbk)
ISBN: 978-1-032-03409-6 (pbk)
ISBN: 978-1-003-18717-2 (ebk)

DOI: 10.1201/9781003187172

Typeset in Caslon
by KnowledgeWorks Global Ltd.

# Contents

FOREWORD                                                          ix

AUTHORS                                                           xiii

GLOSSARY                                                          xv

K-12 RESOURCES                                                    xxi

INTRODUCTION                                                      xxiii

CHAPTER 1    WHY YOU SHOULD READ THIS BOOK                        1
             How We Plan to Present This?                         2
             But First: An Overview of the Contents of the CSEC   3
             The Beginning of the Story: Tom Is Handed a Challenge 4

CHAPTER 2    GETTING DOWN TO BUSINESS: DATA SECURITY              19
             Topic One: Why Is Data Security Important?           20
             The Basic Elements of Data Security: Processing,
             Transmitting, and Storing                            23
             Ensuring Secure Data Transmission: Secure Transmission
             Protocols                                            29
             Ensuring Secure Data Storage: Information Storage Security  33
             Making Data Indecipherable: Cryptology               37
             Cracking the Code: Cryptanalysis                     41
             Forensics: The Investigative Aspect                  43
             Privacy: Ensuring Personal Data                      46

CHAPTER 3    SOFTWARE SECURITY: SOFTWARE UNDERLIES
             EVERYTHING                                           49
             Topic One: Fundamental Principles of Software Security  54
             Thinking about Security in Design                    55

Building the Software Securely                                      57
Assuring the Security of the Software                              58
Secure Deployment and Maintenance                                 61
Ensuring Proper Documentation                                     64
Software Security and Ethics                                      66

CHAPTER 4    COMPONENT SECURITY: IT ALL STARTS WITH
             COMPONENTS                                            71
Designing Secure Components                                       73
Assuring the Architecture: Component Testing                      76
Buying Components Instead of Making Them                          80
The Mystery of Reverse Engineering                               82

CHAPTER 5    CONNECTION SECURITY                                  85
The CSEC Connection Security Knowledge Areas                     89
Topic One: The Physical Components of the Network                89
Topic Two: Physical Interfaces and Connectors                    91
Topic Three: Physical Architecture: The Tangible Part of
the Network                                                       94
Topic Four: Building a Distributed System                        98
Topic Five: Building a Network                                   104
Topic Six: The Bits and Pieces of Network Operation             107
Top Seven: The Practical Considerations of Building a
Network                                                          111
Top Eight: Network Defense                                      115

CHAPTER 6    SYSTEM SECURITY: ASSEMBLING THE PARTS INTO
             A USEFUL WHOLE                                      119
Topic One: Thinking Systematically                              122
Topic Two: Managing What You Create                             125
Topic Three: Controlling Access                                 129
Topic Four: Defending Your System                               133
Topic Five: Retiring an Old System Securely                     138
Topic Six: System Testing                                       138
Topic Seven: Common System Architectures                        141

CHAPTER 7    HUMAN SECURITY: HUMAN-CENTERED THREATS              145
Topic One: Identity Management                                  148
Topic Two: Social Engineering                                   150
Topic Three: Personal Compliance                                154
Topic Four: Awareness and Understanding                         157
Topic Five: Social and Behavioral Privacy                       158
Topic Six: Personal Data Privacy and Security                   161
Topic Seven: Usable Security and Privacy                        163

CHAPTER 8    ORGANIZATIONAL SECURITY: INTRODUCTION
             SECURING THE ENTERPRISE                             167
Topic One: Risk Management                                      169
Topic Two: Security Management                                  172

Topic Three: Cybersecurity Planning                                    175
Topic Four: Business Continuity, Disaster Recovery, and
Incident Management                                                     177
Topic Five: Personnel Security                                         179
Topic Six: Systems Management                                          180
Topic Seven: Security Program Management                               182
Topic Eight: Security Operations Management                            184
Topic Nine: Analytical Tools                                           185

CHAPTER 9    SOCIETAL SECURITY: SECURITY AND SOCIETY                    187
Topic One: Cybercrime                                                  189
Topic Two: Cyber Law                                                   191
Topic Three: Cyber Ethics                                              194
Topic Four: Cyber Policy                                               196
Topic Five: Privacy                                                    198

# Foreword

*Courage is fear in action!* Cybersecurity education needs a whole lot of courage! But the security of our digital world requires that we have to act *now*!

Cybersecurity is all about protecting our digital world. We are woefully short of cybersecurity professionals with a gap of almost 600,000 based on www.cyberseek.org (March 2022). That number keeps growing; it has nearly doubled in four years. As a nation, we are hopeful of transitioning professionals in computer-related fields to cybersecurity, and we should also be *educating* the next generation of digital world defenders. Cybersecurity education does not fit into the traditional middle school or high school models. Yet, it is so important that it needs to find a way to be included in as many educational settings as possible.

I see myself as a cybersecurity "champion" who keeps pushing to get our classes and cyber teams' resources, support, and permissions. This book is for cybersecurity teachers – I challenge you to take on the mantle of cybersecurity champion at your school and in your community.

Cyber champions need to have a sharable vision of what is possible, be willing to keep knocking on doors until you get a few to open, ensure that students are safe and school resources are appropriately protected and spread the news far and wide. Who is the best person for such a champion? There is no stereotype; every community, school district, and school is unique. But, starting at the top with the school district leadership or school principal helps give new program legs. Parents can also really make things happen especially if you advocate for your child who is just starting at a school. The longer a parent can support a school, the better the long-term prognosis. Teachers can also make things happen, as in my case.

Champions need to have a different "elevator" pitch for each group they are trying to persuade school leadership, parents, and students. When my district superintendent practiced what I call "leadership by walking around," he popped into my classroom. I showed him the cyberseek.org website, and he was swift to understand that my program was offering his graduates jobs and promised me whatever support I needed. In the past three years, four of our graduates have been hired to be cybersecurity professionals based on their high school experience – Dr. Scambray was right!

For the teacher who reads this book, the first thing to realize is that you know more about cybersecurity than anyone else on campus. Even if you knew nothing and were voluntold to teach a cyber class, your interest in and experience with technology are great starting points. You and your students will be learning a lot. I explained how guinea pigs were often used to experiment with various things, and then I stated that each was a guinea pig and that I was the head guinea pig. Some days were going to be exceptional, while others would not be nearly as effective. That is okay and expected when you explore a new field of education.

Other cybersecurity teachers created a faint cybersecurity education path, so you do not have to blaze your pathway. I was on two brand new ships during my twenty-one years as a Sailor. In both cases, we never tried to create anything ourselves. In a similar vein, you will find other teachers who will help. I am certainly happy to share *all* of my teaching experiences and *most* of my competition tips. (Troy Cyber's secret sauce that has created multiple national cybersecurity champions will remain a secret.)

I have taught high school since 2005 in California. So I am very familiar with the California education requirements for high school students; most states have similar standards. It is impractical to expect that we will somehow add cybersecurity as yet another graduation requirement. Education tends to be a zero-sum game; a class needs to be dropped if you add a course. But there are still ways to include cybersecurity as an option for some students. We need to be innovative and find areas where we can:

1. Incorporate cybersecurity lessons into existing lessons.
2. Create electives for students to experience cybersecurity first hand.
3. Start after-school cybersecurity programs like CyberPatriot.
4. Offer summer cybersecurity camps.
5. Look for new ideas based on lessons learned for all of these options.

Does this sound too ambitious? We are doing *all* of these at Troy High School in Fullerton, California. None of these happened quickly; they are the result of twelve years of good intentions, missteps, having myself and students acting as guinea pigs as we tried different curricula, ideas, labs to find what worked and what did not.

We started with five students in 2010 and found that they liked learning about cybersecurity, and soon others wanted to join in. In 2015, we offered our local middle school the opportunity to have some of their students join us after school for our twice-weekly cyber practice. In September, what started as five 7th and 8th grades, we became twenty by December. Our school leadership took notice when I gave them an update. Certainly, seeing a middle schooler in a high school classroom is already a success story; they see the "next level" of education. But these students were learning about hardening Windows and Linux computers, a skill usually reserved for upper-division college students in the mid-2010s. These thirteen- and fourteen-year-olds enjoyed learning from high school students and were not intimidated. In addition, I noticed that a higher percentage of females came from middle school; this is another huge reason to offer cybersecurity education at the middle school level.

Troy High School decided to offer a pathway for the 2016–2017 school year. It is time to transform other schools into Troy-like. It is not about the number of students. What matters is passion and quality of instruction and allowing ALL students to see if "Cyber is their thing."

The Troy model treats cyber as a sport. We have try-outs, summer camps, regular weekly practices, team rosters, varsity letters, letter jackets, end-of-season banquet, inclusion in the school's morning announcements, a page in the yearbook, and our national achievements painted outside of our classroom. Many of these things made sense, but others were inspired by our students, parents, and vision. I challenge others to follow our lead!

Thank you to Dan and Tamara Shoemaker and Ken Sigler for this book that I hope will inspire a brand-new group of cybersecurity educators and give you the courage to open those closed doors.

**Allen Stubblefield**

*Cybersecurity and IT teacher, Troy High School, Fullerton, California*
*Head Cybersecurity Coach, Troy Cyber, Fullerton, California*

# Authors

**Daniel Shoemaker, PhD,** is a distinguished visitor of the IEEE, full professor, senior research scientist, and program director at the University of Detroit Mercy's Center for Cyber Security and Intelligence Studies. Dan is a former chair of the Cybersecurity and Information Systems Department and has authored numerous books and journal articles focused on cybersecurity.

**Ken Sigler** is a faculty member of the Computer Information Systems (CIS) program and Chair of Curriculum Instruction at Oakland Community College in Michigan. Ken's research is in the areas of software management, software assurance, cybersecurity management and cybersecurity education in which he has published several books and articles.

**Tamara Shoemaker** is Director for Cyber Security and Intelligence Studies at the University of Detroit Mercy. She spearheaded the development of two university department's community outreach and development strategy, CIS (cybersecurity programs) and the criminal justice (CJ and intelligence analysis). Tamara coordinates projects with government entities, academic organizations, industry and law enforcement agencies locally, nationally and internationally.

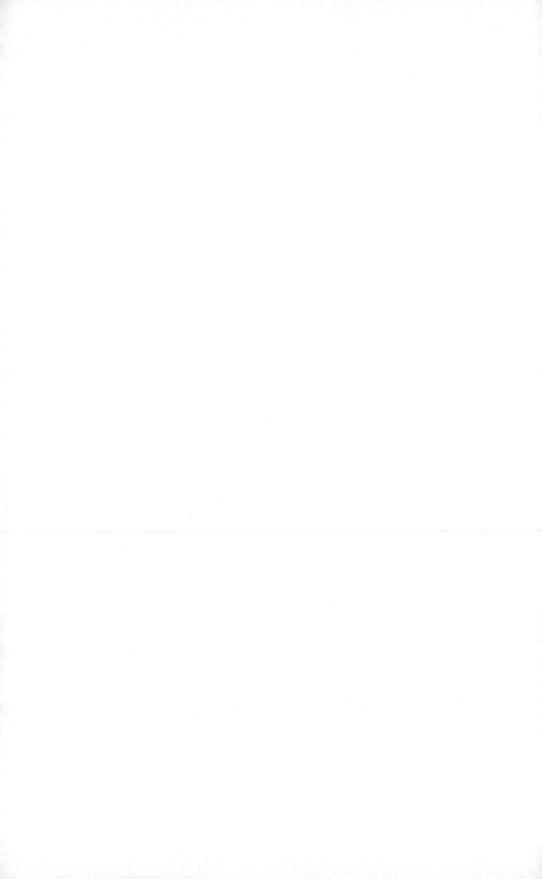

# Glossary

## Cyberecurity Terms You Are Likely to Encounter

**Access control:** the process of granting or denying a request to obtain information, or related services.

**Access control mechanism:** a measure designed to detect and deny unauthorized access and permit authorized access.

**Adversary:** any individual, group, organization, or government that conducts or has the intent to conduct detrimental activities.

**Attack:** any attempt to gain unauthorized access to system services, resources, or information, or an attempt to compromise system integrity.

**Attack method:** the manner or technique an adversary uses to attack information or a system.

**Attack surface:** the access points by which an adversary can enter a system to cause harm.

**Attacker:** the individual, group, organization, or government that executes an attack.

**Authentication:** the process of verifying the identity or other attributes of an entity.

**Authorization:** a process of determining whether a subject is allowed to have the specified types of access to a particular resource.

**Availability:** the property of being accessible and usable upon demand.

**Ciphertext:** data or information in its encrypted form.

**Computer forensics:** the actions taken to defend against unauthorized activity within computer networks.

**Confidentiality:** a condition where information is not disclosed to users, processes, or devices unless they have been authorized to access the information.

**Cryptography:** the use of mathematical techniques to provide security services.

**Cybersecurity:** an activity or process whereby systems and information are protected from and/or defended against damage, unauthorized use or modification, or exploitation.

**Data integrity:** the property that data is complete, intact, and trusted and has not been modified or destroyed in an unauthorized or accidental manner.

**Data mining:** a process or technique used to analyze large sets of existing information to discover previously unrevealed patterns or correlations.

**Denial of service:** an attack that prevents or impairs the authorized use of system. resources or services.

**Digital forensics:** the processes and specialized techniques for gathering, retaining, and analyzing system-related data (digital evidence) for investigative purposes.

**Digital signature:** a value computed with a cryptographic process and then appended to a data object, thereby digitally signing the data.

**Distributed denial of service:** a technique that uses numerous systems to perform a simultaneous attack.

**Encryption:** the process of transforming plaintext into ciphertext.

**Exploit:** a technique to breach the security of a network or system in violation of security policy.

**Exposure:** the condition of being unprotected, thereby allowing access to an attacker.

**Firewall:** a capability to limit network traffic between networks and/ or information systems.

**Identity and access management:** the methods and processes used to manage subjects and their authentication and authorizations to access specific objects.

**Incident:** a occurrence that results in adverse consequences that may require action to mitigate.

**Incident response:** the activities that address the short-term, direct effects of an incident.

**Information assurance:** measures that protect and defend information and information systems.

**Information technology:** any equipment or interconnected system or subsystem of equipment that processes, transmits, receives, or interchanges data or information.

**Insider threat:** a person or group of persons within an organization who pose a potential risk due to trusted access.

**Integrity:** the property whereby information, an information system, or a component of a system has not been modified or destroyed in an unauthorized manner.

**Intrusion:** the act of bypassing the security mechanisms of a network or information system.

**Intrusion detection:** techniques for analyzing networks and information systems to determine if a security breach or security violation has occurred.

**Malicious code:** programming intended to perform an unauthorized function that will have adverse impact on the confidentiality, integrity, or availability of an information system.

**Malware:** software that harms the operation of a system by performing an unauthorized function.

**Mitigation:** the application of one or more measures to reduce the likelihood of an unwanted occurrence and/or lessen its consequences.

**Non-repudiation:** a cryptographic method to prevent an individual or entity from falsely denying a computerized action that was taken.

**Object:** a discreet information system-related entity containing or receiving information.

**Password:** a string of characters (letters, numbers, and other symbols) used to authenticate an identity or to verify access authorization.

**Penetration testing:** a method where testers search for vulnerabilities and then try to attack them in order to test its access management and resilience.

**Phishing:** a digital form of social engineering to deceive individuals into providing sensitive information.

**Privacy:** the assurance that the confidentiality of, and access to, certain information about an entity is protected.

**Public key infrastructure:** a framework consisting of standards and services to enable secure, encrypted communication and authentication over potentially insecure networks.

**Response:** activities that address the short-term, direct effects of an incident, and may also support short-term recovery.

**Risk:** the potential for an unwanted or adverse outcome resulting from an incident, event, or occurrence, based on the likelihood that a particular threat will exploit a particular vulnerability

**Risk analysis:** systematic assessment of the components and characteristics of risk.

**Risk assessment:** the product or process which collects information and assigns values to risks.

**Risk management:** the process of identifying, analyzing, assessing, and communicating risk.

**Software assurance:** the level of confidence that software is free from vulnerabilities, either intentionally designed into the software or accidentally inserted at any time during its lifecycle.

**Spoofing:** faking the sending address of a transmission to gain unauthorized access.

**Supply chain risk management:** the process of assessing supply chain risk and controlling it to an acceptable level of risk investment.

**Systems development:** the action of moving a system through the various phases of the development lifecycle.

**Test and evaluation:** conduct of tests to evaluate compliance with specifications and requirements and validation of technical, functional, and performance characteristics.

**Threat:** a circumstance or event that has or indicates the potential to exploit vulnerabilities and to adversely impact operations, or assets.

**Threat actor:** an agent of threat.

**Threat analysis:** detailed evaluation of the characteristics of individual threats.

**Threat assessment:** a process of identifying or evaluating entities, actions, or occurrences, that have or indicate the potential to harm life, information, operations, and/or property.

**Virus:** a computer program that can replicate itself, infect a computer without permission or knowledge of the user, and then spread or propagate to another computer.

**Vulnerability:** a characteristic or specific weakness that renders an organization or asset open to exploitation by a given threat or susceptible to a given hazard.

**Weakness:** a defect or imperfection in software code, design, architecture, or deployment that, under proper conditions, could become a vulnerability or contribute to the introduction of vulnerabilities.

**Worm:** a self-replicating, self-propagating, self-contained program that uses networking mechanisms to spread itself.

# K-12 Resources

| | |
|---|---|
| Bandit Waregame (Game) | http://overthewire.org/wargames/bandit/ |
| "Reverse Engineering for Beginners" free book | http://beginners.re/ |
| Capture the Flag Competitions | https://github.com/isislab/Project-Ideas/wiki/Capture-The-Flag-Competitions |
| Capture the Flag Events | https://ctftime.org/ |
| Capture the Flag Field Guide | https://trailofbits.github.io/ctf/ |
| Capture the Flag Practice List | http://captf.com/practice-ctf/ |
| Cipher Tools | http://rumkin.com/tools/cipher/ |
| Clip Training – Social Engineering (Lesson 1) The Art of Deception | https://www.youtube.com/watch?v=xn9hH1BckPE |
| Code | https://code.org/ |
| Code Combat (Game) | https://codecombat.com/ |
| Coursera | https://www.coursera.org/ |
| Cyber Aces – Free online security courses | http://www.cyberaces.org/ |
| CyberPatriot | https://www.uscyberpatriot.org/ |
| Day of Cyber | http://www.nsadayofcyber.com/ |
| Empowering Educators to Teach Cyber – Free Cyber Curriculum | https://cyber.org/ |
| Full Stack Python – Web Application Security | https://www.fullstackpython.com/web-application-security.html |
| iKeepSafe – Online Privacy Training | http://ikeepsafe.org/ |

| | |
|---|---|
| Kahoot | https://getkahoot.com/ |
| Khan Academy – Caesar Cipher | https://www.youtube.com/watch?v=sMOZf4GN3oc&feature=youtu.be |
| Khan Academy – The Internet: Cybersecurity and Crime | https://www.youtube.com/watch?v=5k24We8pED8 |
| Media Smarts Educational Games | http://mediasmarts.ca/digital-media-literacy/educational-games |
| Metasploit Unleashed – Free Online Security Training | https://www.offensive-security.com/metasploit-unleashed/ |
| MIT App Inventor | http://appinventor.mit.edu/explore/ |
| NOVALABS Cybersecurity Lab (Game) | https://www.pbs.org/wgbh/nova/labs/lab/cyber/ |
| Open Source Cyber Security Learning | https://www.cybrary.it/ |
| OWASP AppSec Tutorial Series – teaches application security | https://www.owasp.org/index.php/OWASP_Appsec_Tutorial_Series |
| Penetration Testing | https://pentesterlab.com/ |
| Pentest Class – Reverse Engineering 1 | https://www.youtube.com/watch?v=cATBah30jk0 |
| Raspberry Pi | https://www.raspberrypi.org/ |
| Reverse Engineering Resources | https://pewpewthespells.com/re.html |
| Scratch Programming Activities | https://scratch.mit.edu/ |
| TekDefense – TekTip ep1 – Basic Dynamic Malware Analysis | https://www.youtube.com/watch?v=2YQ2KqZ4gbo |
| The OSI Model Animation | https://www.youtube.com/watch?v=-6Uoku-M6oY |
| The OSI Model's Seven Layers Defined and Function Explained | https://support.microsoft.com/en-us/kb/103884 |
| Top 10 Secure Coding Practices | https://www.securecoding.cert.org/confluence/display/seccode/Top+10+Secure+Coding+Practices |
| Unix/Linux Command Reference | https://files.fosswire.com/2007/08/fwunixref.pdf |
| Wireshark Tutorial for Beginners 2015 | https://www.youtube.com/watch?v=TkCSr30UojM |

---

CSEC 2017: https://cybered.acm.org/

# Introduction

## Teaching Cybersecurity

### Introduction: We Need to Know What to Teach

I'm a teacher, just like you are. And so I know that the first requirement for any course is its subject matter. That's the reason why I wrote this book. Its contents are based on the ACM/IEEE common body of knowledge for cybersecurity which was created and sanctioned by the organizations that have customarily dictated curricular content for the computing fields. Those societies usually focus on their specific areas of interest. However, they will occasionally come together to publish cross-disciplinary recommendations for a topic of vital mutual interest. That is the case here.

Over the past decade, it has become clear that the things that ought to be taught in a cybersecurity class are more or less in the eye of the beholder. So the societies created a single universally recognized field concept. Its official title is "Cybersecurity Curricula 2017, Curricular Volume." But it is colloquially called CSEC2017. The CSEC2017 aims to serve as "*The leading resource for comprehensive cybersecurity curricular content for global academic institutions seeking to develop a broad range of cybersecurity offerings at the post-secondary level*" (CSEC 2017 Mission Statement). That vision is what motivates this book.

### The Things You Will Learn by Reading This

The mastery of course content is the first requirement for competent teaching. CSEC2017 provides that knowledge. It was specifically designed for higher education and the profession. Thus, this book gives you, the teacher, a complete and easy-to-follow discussion of the CSEC's topics. We've packaged it so that a senior high school and junior high school teacher can easily understand it.

Hence, unlike the more heavyweight professional books, our focus is strictly on the various ways that the body of knowledge can be delivered within a conventional secondary school classroom. As a result, there will be no deep dives into the gory details of any topic. Instead, we will emphasize practical ways to ensure that your students can understand and relate to the field's diverse facets. We also provide model delivery suggestions that will help you facilitate that understanding. In that respect, then, this book is a simple, comprehensive teacher's handbook for the field of cybersecurity, with all of its topics packaged for practical teaching purposes at the secondary level.

Because we expect you, the teacher, to have little or no background in cybersecurity or even in computing as a whole, we have sought to keep the presentation as down-to-earth and relatable as possible. Consequently, all of this material will be presented through an end-to-end story that will call out the practical issues as you might view them from your classroom. The aim is to help an inexperienced reader see how the field's contents fit together within a real-world application. So, this offers a general understanding of the commonly accepted body of knowledge without any unnecessary in-depth details or technical jargon. It also provides easy-to-apply teaching suggestions for each of the areas. Teaching materials will include illustrations, examples, exercises, and shared resources for each topic.

### Advantages of This Book

This book offers the most authoritative content possible, not just the opinions of individual "experts." The role of the governing societies for the profession is well-established. Thus, these recommendations are authoritative. However, the book's distinctiveness lies in our specific intent to provide you, the traditional classroom teacher, with all of the knowledge and tools you will need to deliver a comprehensive course in cybersecurity. In that respect, then, the contents of this book should be viewed as the map that traditional K-12 districts can use to lay out a complete course on that topic. The book itself is holistic because it covers the entire formal body of knowledge. However, individual classroom teachers will be given sufficient guidance to help them fit their particular situation into the overall perspective.

## Table of Contents

**Chapter 1: Tom and Lucy Meet the Doc** – this is a short introduction and orientation to why a common body of knowledge is essential. The arrival of the computer societies on the scene and their role is explained. We also introduce our three intrepid explorers: Tom, who teaches a high school computer course, Lucy, who does the same thing at the junior high level, and the Doc, an odd old fellow who appears to have just wandered in to advise them. At the end of this chapter, you will understand why a comprehensive body of knowledge for cybersecurity is essential, and you will know why it is vital to get it into your classroom.

**Chapter 2: Knowledge Area One – Data Security** – all of the succeeding eight chapters will have the same format. Knowledge units and topics will be laid out and discussed by our three adventurers. The Data Security knowledge area focuses on every aspect of data protection. Thus, the discussion will center on access control, data protection through encryption, and database security.

**Chapter 3: Knowledge Area Two – Software Security** – the software security knowledge area focuses on the development and use of the software. Consequently, the discussion will center on secure software development, implementation, testing, patching, and the ethics of software operation and use.

**Chapter 4: Knowledge Area Three-Component Security** – the component security knowledge area focuses on the components integrated into larger systems. Thus, the discussion will center on the various aspects of system component security.

**Chapter 5: Knowledge Area Four – Connection Security** – the connection security knowledge area focuses on the interconnections between components, including physical and logical connectors. This is the traditional network security area. So, the discussion will center on the curricular elements of teaching networking and types of transmission and connection attacks.

**Chapter 6: Knowledge Area Five – System Security** – the system security knowledge area focuses on recommendations regarding a holistic approach to security policy and access control. Along with that, we will discuss system monitoring and recovery.

**Chapter 7: Knowledge Area Six – Human Security** – the human security knowledge area focuses on human behavior related to cybersecurity. There will be discussions about how to teach identity management, social engineering, awareness and understanding, and personal data privacy and security. This is one of the areas that are pioneering additions to the body of knowledge.

**Chapter 8: Knowledge Area Seven – Organizational Security** – the organizational security knowledge area focuses on how organizations protect themselves from cybersecurity threats, as well as the management of risk. Consequently, the discussion will center on the traditional areas of strategy, organizational risk management, governance and policy, laws, ethics, and compliance.

**Chapter 9: Knowledge Area Eight – Societal Security** – the societal security knowledge area focuses on aspects of cybersecurity that broadly impact society as a whole, such as cybercrime, law, ethics, policy, privacy, and their relation to each other. This is another groundbreaking area in the model.

Our aim in all this is to help you connect the dots between the contents of the cybersecurity body of knowledge and your teaching strategies.

# 1

# WHY YOU SHOULD READ THIS BOOK

This book provides advice and guidance you will need to teach cybersecurity in a grade 7–12 classroom. The problem is that cybersecurity is a new field, and understandably, there are conflicting ideas about how to teach it. That's why it is so important to base your teaching on a commonly accepted body of knowledge. That common body of knowledge is titled CSEC2017 Curriculum Guidelines for Post-Secondary Degree Programs. The CSEC is called that because its recommendations were initially created for post-secondary education. However, the CSEC successfully itemize the generic principles for the field. Therefore, it can be a reliable basis for building a cybersecurity course. This is good news for grade 7–12 educators because those principles can support the teaching of cybersecurity at their level.

The CSEC gets its legitimacy from the fact that it was developed under the auspices of the three professional organizations that formally oversee computing: The Association for Computer Machinery (ACM), the Institute of Electrical and Electronic Engineers (IEEE), and the Association for Information Systems (IAS). These groups sponsor the academic fields of computer science, software engineering, and business information systems. They occasionally come together as a body-of-the-whole to develop and disseminate recommendations about topics of significant interest to the profession. The CSEC is one of the two documents of that type. It expresses the profession's consensus view of the appropriate contents for cybersecurity, and as a result, the CSEC provides a substantive basis for building a curriculum.

Even so, we have to pause for a minute here to make an important distinction. In practice, the National Institute of Standards and Technology's Cybersecurity Workforce Framework (NICE) offers a set of commonly accepted recommendations about the requirements

DOI: 10.1201/9781003187172-1

for cybersecurity work. In that respect, it dictates the "what," while CSEC supplies the "why." The distinction between "what" and "why" is important because teachers want to ensure their students' real-world success with the instruction they provide. So, those are the "what." But it is also essential to understand how those skills apply in practice. That is the "why." A fully informed person understands both things in tandem, so knowing both the CSEC and the NICE Framework is crucial.

Each chapter in this book will present one of the eight knowledge areas of the CSEC. The goal is to complete a basic understanding of the field, not dive into the details. That will come later in the educational process. We aim to give you a comprehensive look at all of the fundamental concepts that comprise the discipline of cybersecurity. Thus, this book is the first step in a long voyage to mastering the realm of cybersecurity.

### How We Plan to Present This?

Cybersecurity is far too broad a field to encompass in a single text. Therefore, this book will provide a practical overview of the essential elements of the field without getting into the nuts-and-bolts of each of the CSEC's knowledge areas. That detail is for later learning. Instead, we will summarize each knowledge area using a simple, understandable conversation. In the interaction of the characters, we hope to provide a roadmap for readers that will let them build a personal understanding of the body of knowledge and decide how to adapt its concepts to their particular instructional needs.

The unique aspect of this book is that the eight content areas are illustrated and discussed in an easy-to-read story. The story itself will be kept generic, without specifics or technical jargon. More pertinently, we will provide several easy-to-administer exercises for each knowledge area. It should be understood that, as a disciplinary model, the CSEC comprises a unified framework, one that fully embodies all of the elements of the field. However, individual teachers will be given sufficient guidance to decide where to add their specialized interests into the course – for instance, personal interests such as coding, networks, or even ethics.

It is important to note that this book is not a conventional text-book. The discussion of the subject matter occurs entirely within a story, which we hope will entertain and help you see how you can apply the CSEC in a particular situation. The story follows a typical process for structuring a new course in a real-world education setting. The narrative will be told through the eyes of two familiar educators, both of whom are classroom teachers in a traditional school district. Our heroes have just been handed the unwelcome assignment of creating a brand-new course in cybersecurity for their district's high school and junior high students. An expert in cybersecurity education will help in their efforts along the way. He will provide the general context, guidance, and occasional comic relief.

Our little tale will illustrate the everyday things that people might need to consider in building a course in cybersecurity at the secondary school level. It will also introduce the fundamental knowledge units that an average teacher needs to incorporate to be complete. This general understanding will ensure that your students are aware of all the aspects of cybersecurity. Finally, the reader will see how our heroes delve into the diverse elements of the body of knowledge and see them wrestle with the current problems the field faces. By the end of this book, the reader will understand how to teach cybersecurity properly. In addition, you will know about the common pitfalls that a person might face in designing a genuinely complete course in cybersecurity.

**But First: An Overview of the Contents of the CSEC**

There are five explicitly technical areas in the CSEC body of knowledge. These traditional areas are (1) Data Security, (2) Software Security, (3) Component Security, (4) Connection Security, and (5) System Security. The **Data Security** knowledge area entails data protection topics centered on cryptography, digital forensics, and the assurance of data integrity. **Software Security** comprises the traditional lifecycle of software. That chapter will cover security requirements, security design, testing, configuring, and patching software. **Component Security** focuses on the design, procurement, testing, analysis, and maintenance of sub-components of larger systems. It also introduces the knotty issue of supply chain security. The **Connection Security** knowledge area involves the familiar topics of traditional network security. Finally, **System Security** focuses on the assurance of systems. The discussion centers on ways to integrate these five areas into an effective high-level understanding of that aspect of the field.

There are also three explicitly behavioral areas in the body of knowledge. These three represent the truly unique feature of the CSEC. Although they are not strictly computer-based, the attacks originating from human and physical sources now encompass most of the losses and data comprises. That is why topics like insider attacks, social engineering, and phishing are of great interest to the profession. The three quasi-behavioral areas are: (1) Human Security, (2) Organizational Security, and (3) Societal Security. The **Human Security** knowledge area focuses on ensuring the trustworthiness of people. Hence, topics include such human-centered activities as identity management, social engineering, and personal data privacy and security protection. The **Organizational Security** area focuses on managing enterprise risk exposure to ensure the business's goals. Consequently, the topics in this area center on processes such as risk management, policy governance, and compliance with laws and regulations. Finally, the **Societal Security** knowledge area focuses on society as a whole. Consequently, topics in this area include cyber law, cyber ethics, cyber policy, and privacy and how they all relate to each other.

Now that we've gotten the disclaimers out of the way, the remainder of this book is built around a story that illustrates how a typical classroom teacher might adapt the cybersecurity common body of knowledge to their particular needs. We realize that most reference books are built around facts, not fiction. But we also believe that showing is better than telling. So, although the facts are there, we will try to present them in the way that an educator is likely to have to think about them. As a result, the story itself might seem a bit inconsequential. But the message that it conveys will give you a much more personal view of how ordinary people might approach this critical issue.

### The Beginning of the Story: Tom Is Handed a Challenge

Our story begins at the end of June. Even though most teachers are out of school, that's when every one of us begins our lesson planning for the following year. Tom, our hero, had just gotten his tenure at the high school, and he was looking forward to his new job as the district's first IT instructor. In addition to his major in education and his teaching certificate, Tom also had a minor in information technology from his college's business school. He taught Perl, Python, and networks during his three-year probationary period.

Tom was thinking about new and better ways to approach IT teaching when he got a polite note from the District Office asking him to drop by to chat with the Superintendent. Tom might have been a mere twenty-five year old, but he was an ambitious young fellow, and he was delighted at the opportunity to present his ideas to the boss. Hence, he appeared bright and early the very next morning at the Superintendent's office, hair neatly combed and dressed in his best suit.

The Superintendent was an older fellow who'd been with the district so long that the teaching staff thought he'd come with the buildings. So after exchanging the usual niceties, the Superintendent got down to business. He said, "I've had some excellent reports about you, Tom. You're smart, hardworking, and innovative, and that's the sort of attitude we like around here."

That was good news. Tom blushed and said self-effacingly, "I just want to do a good job, Sir." The Superintendent added, "That's the reason why I selected you for a special assignment." There was something in the way the Superintendent said the last part, which set off alarm bells in Tom's head. He leaned back in his chair and sounded a bit warily, "What can I do for you, Sir?"

The Superintendent said, "The Board of Education has been bugging me to get cybersecurity teaching into the schools. Those people are mostly businessmen, and they say that it's important stuff for them - something that they all need. The problem is that they can't seem to tell me exactly what it is or what we're supposed to teach."

The Superintendent added, "Now, I taught English when I was your age." Tom thought to himself, "He probably knew Shakespeare personally," but he remained attentive. The Superintendent was still talking, "I know what an English curriculum is supposed to contain because the conventions haven't changed in hundreds of years. But there doesn't seem to be any person in our district, or on the Board itself, who can agree about what should be taught in a cybersecurity course. I get a whole bunch of conflicting ideas.

Some people say it's just coding. Some call it computer science; others tell me it involves networking too. We even have a few people who say it's bigger than all that, something called NICE. So that's where you come in. I don't want an opinion; I want proof. I want you to research and design a course for us that is based on something real and legitimate, not somebody's opinion, something that I can take to the Board to prove beyond a shadow that we are teaching the right thing."

Tom was watching his summer vacation morph into an eternity of time on the internet. But he said, trying to sound eager, "That's a great opportunity, Sir! I'm looking forward to getting started." The Superintendent stood and shook Tom's hand as he said, "That's the right attitude, my boy. I knew we made the right choice when we decided to tenure you." At the same time, the Superintendent was thinking, "Every young whippersnapper needs to spend a little time in the salt mines; it makes them appreciate what they've got."

The Superintendent added, "You should talk to Lucy over at the Middle School. We've given her the same task for the Junior High kids. I'm sure the two of you can come up with something that we can all be proud of in our District."

**Figure 1.1**   Tom accepts the new opportunity.

Meanwhile, Lucy thought, "Great, one more waste of time!" Lucy had taught the science courses at the Applewood Middle School for the past seventeen years, and she'd seen it all. She had served on committees, task forces, and working groups, all dedicated to some new-fangled flavor of the month in middle school education. They had produced reports, recommendations, even curriculum plans. Every one of them had sunk without a trace. Now, her principal had just handed her one more of "those kinds" of assignments.

He'd told her that she had to work with a wet behind the ears ed-school graduate. The goal was to develop a proposal regarding what to teach in a cybersecurity course. Of course, Lucy had heard about cybersecurity. It sounded like the same sort of craze that had taken precious hours out of her life in the past – like the big push that never happened to close the digital divide. Even the term "cybersecurity" sounded clichéd. Lucy knew that "cyber" meant that it had something to do with computers, and she had been teaching the kids using Raspberry Pi for the past six years. But what was the "security" angle? Were they talking about teaching kids how to secure a computer? That seemed simple enough; just follow the rules and lock it up afterward? Or was it something more complicated?

The first meeting between Tom and Lucy didn't go well. In Lucy's opinion, Tom was about as focused as a squirrel on a busy road and a stone nerd to boot. On the other hand, Tom viewed Lucy as the kind of cynical old crustacean which was always a barrier to progress. Yet they did agree on one thing. They didn't want to reinvent the wheel. So, they tried to base their recommendations on commonly accepted practices.

Of course, Tom and Lucy also knew that most curriculum standards for computing were designed for college teaching. The aim of those standards was to produce a student who was capable of moving directly into practice, while Tom and Lucy's focus was on junior high and high school learners. Even worse, Tom and Lucy's problems were precisely the same as the Superintendents. There was no agreement about what the end product of a K-12 cybersecurity education process ought to look like.

Instead, there was a wilderness of commercial products available for purchase "at a low-low price," all purported to provide everything that a student would need to learn cybersecurity. So naturally, none of these products came close to agreeing with each other. Instead, it seemed like each was designed to make a buck for the perpetrators, not provide a common means of understanding. Of course, they all had a few things in common, like the need for programming and networking knowledge. But it was evident to both Tom and Lucy that none of the commercial products provided a unified top-level vision for the field.

That led Tom and Lucy to explore the question of whether there might be more legitimate recommendations available, the kind that had a bit of traditional authority behind them. Ideally, those recommendations would be backed by a group that customarily provided advice for the profession, such as the groups that wrote the common standards used in professional practice. Tom and Lucy started with the state-level educational standards. Their state had a mandated requirement for teaching "computer science," which was nothing more than straightforward IT content. Unfortunately, there was no national standard for cybersecurity, only recommendations from grant-funded interest groups. Worse, every individual state approached the subject differently. Tom had already reviewed the standard for his state, and it required nothing more than critical thinking exercises. They included algorithms, logic, and the simple things that you would need to know to operate a computer, such as the rudiments of the operating system, networks, and programming. Social issues also got some attention at the higher grades. But there was nothing in their state requirements specifically focused on how to defend a computer or its information from a determined adversary.

So the question remained, where were Tom and Lucy supposed to get trustworthy advice about the appropriate content of an introductory course in cybersecurity? Lucy finally said, "We've always brought in an outside expert whenever we got into an area that none of us knew anything about." That set Tom to thinking. He said tentatively, "I could call up my old college mentor. He's helped me in the past, and he knows a lot of people. Maybe he could recommend somebody who'd be willing to help us."

Lucy thought to herself, "He's such a college boy; the last thing we need is an ivory tower nerd telling us what we ought to teach in a real-world classroom." So, she said sourly, "The district doesn't have money to pay an expert." Lucy thought, "That ought to chase the vulture off." Tom said, "Let me try anyway. My mentor might know somebody who'd advise us just for the good of society."

That was such a preciously naive statement that Lucy laughed out loud. She said, "Hah!!! That'll be the day." But in her mind, she thought, "This kid is just too trusting for words." Yet, Lucy was proven wrong. The next day Tom said beaming, "I talked to a fellow who's willing to help us. Not only that, but he'll be joining us today." Lucy said sourly, "I'll bet he's a real gem." That was the precise point where the door opened, and the oddest-looking man walked in.

He was perhaps seventy, tall, thin, with wire-rimmed glasses and wildly unkempt hair. He was also dressed in an outfit last in vogue when Ronald Reagan was president. The fellow stopped at the door and said, "Are you the young man I talked to yesterday?" Tom said, "I am, Professor." He fetched a chair for the old guy and said to Lucy, "Professor Brown has some ideas that we might use to create a course in cybersecurity, and he's willing to help us out of pure personal interest." As he sat down, the old guy said, "It isn't Professor anymore, just Doc Brown. I couldn't stand the academic rat race. So now I just research and write; it lets me say what I think without having to worry about other people's opinions."

Lucy thought to herself, "Great, Tom's found us the academic equivalent of a loose cannon." But she said, "Not to be rude, but why should we even listen to you." The Doc cackled, pointed at Lucy, and said emphatically, "I like this one." He continued with, "I started with computers in the second generation. We did all of our programming with punch cards, not keyboards. So, I've seen it all, from nine-track tape to the cloud." Then, he added cheerfully, "All those years give you a little bit of perspective. You need to have that to cope with the crazy changes that have happened over the years." The Doc looked at both of them and said significantly, "More important, it doesn't tie you down to existing assumptions."

The Doc continued with, "My colleagues are products of their experience and education. They only know what they've seen, and they think that what they know is the whole truth and nothing but the truth. But computing isn't like any other business when it comes to change." He added, "Anybody over the age of thirty is essentially self-taught. The internet was created thirty years ago, and the way we use it is no more than twenty-five years old. The cloud has been around for fifteen years, and Twitter was launched in 2006. So, if you were educated before 1990 you didn't learn anything relevant to modern computing, and if you graduated in the 1990s, you didn't learn anything about cyberspace. Even worse, if you spent forty years in the field, your formative years were spent developing a set of assumptions that simply don't apply at all to the brave new world of the internet."

Lucy spluttered, "Now look here! I'm as competent as anybody else when it comes to the internet. You don't have to go to school to know how to use Facebook." The Doc gave Lucy an amused glance and said, "Really? You might be able to do many things on your computer, and you might be a real whiz when it comes to finding and using new applications. But do you truly understand the integrated, the highly interdependent, and cross-cutting virtual world that those applications operate in, or have you thought about the profound changes to society and humanity that global interconnectedness has created?"

Lucy said huffily, "Of course not, and why should I!! Cyberspace is way too complicated to know what's going on behind the curtain. Most people don't even know what they ought to know." The Doc raised his eyebrows and said, "Don't you think that it's a bit dangerous to trust everything that you value, from your privacy to your bank account to something that you don't have a clue how to protect. After all, the internet is the single most significant influence on human society since movable type. So, you can master the basic principles of cybersecurity or become a helpless victim. It's your choice."

The Doc added kindly, "To be fair though, the two of you are taking the first important steps in ensuring that your students understand threat and risk in the virtual environment." Lucy said, "What the heck are you talking about – threat and risk? What does that have to do with teaching cybersecurity?"

The Doc chuckled and said, "the first commercially built computers have been around since 1950. Of course, they've gotten infinitely more capable over the ensuing seventy years. But the fundamental concepts laid down by folks like Turing and Von Neuman haven't changed. Computers still manipulate stored data through a linear process. What HAS changed is the ubiquity of things. They were once million-dollar, three-story dinosaurs that required a scientist to operate them. Now kids have more computing power in their pants pocket than all computing devices that existed in the 1950s. And thanks to interconnectedness, our modern society can't survive without interacting virtually."

He added, "Think of it, how much of your daily life depends on the ability to communicate and process data. Everything from entertaining ourselves to our national infrastructure sits on a virtual platform. And so, society as we know it would descend into total chaos if we took that capability away." The Doc paused to let that point sink in. Then he added meaningfully, "We've always had threats to computers. But until the internet, those were limited to the individual device. Now that we've hooked them all together, we have created something called the adversary."

Lucy said, "What in the heck is an adversary? I mean, I know what the word means, but why is it relevant to our discussion?" The Doc said, sounding pleased, "That's a great question, Lucy. The adversary is that faceless entity who lurks out there in cyberspace, waiting to violate the confidentiality, integrity, and availability of your computerized transactions. We currently lose upwards of two TRILLION dollars a year to those people. That's the gross national product of England and France. But even worse, that same bad guy could cause a life extinguishing event, like the destruction of our electrical power grid, that would return us to the Dark Ages."

Both Tom and Lucy sat there with their mouths hanging open. Finally, Tom said, "But surely if the danger's that obvious, then we've done something to address the problem. I mean, we've had some incredible breakthroughs like artificial intelligence. Won't the continuous advance of technology save us?" The Doc said tartly, "The continuous advance of technology is more likely to do us in. Let me tell you a little tale." Lucy thought, "This guy has the attention span of a golden retriever!! First, he tries to scare us to death, and now he wants to tell us a story."

The Doc said, "There's an old poem about six blind men and an elephant. The way the story goes, six blind men were asked to describe an elephant based on the part they were touching. So the guy touching the tusk said it was a spear and the one touching the trunk thought it was a snake. The one touching the ear described it as a leaf; the one touching the side thought it was a wall, the one touching the leg thought it was a tree. Finally, the guy holding the tail thought it was a rope." The Doc paused, looked at the two of them meaningfully, and said, "The point is that it was reasonable to assume that they knew what an elephant looked like, based on what they were touching. But every one of them was wrong." Both Lucy and Tom stared at the Doc with dawning comprehension.

The Doc added, "That's the situation with cybersecurity today. Some elements of the field are very advanced. But they only address part of the problem. And of course, if all of the relevant aspects of the problem aren't completely or uniformly addressed, that will cause gaps in any protection scheme. If a gap exists, all the adversary has to do is find it and exploit it. That's every hacker's game plan. They know that there will always be a hole in any defense."

Tom said, "So, what should we do? There's no way we can ensure a reliable security solution if we don't address all the parts of the problem. How do we break down the existing stovepipes?" The Doc looked at Tom with newfound respect; maybe the kid was smarter than he'd initially thought. The Doc said, "The profession is aware of the necessity for comprehensive protection. They even have a term for it, 'holistic.' But the people who call the shots in academia, government, and industry all seem to be fighting the last war."

Both Tom and Lucy looked like they didn't understand what he'd just said. So, the Doc added, let me explain, "For the first thirty years of the field, the problem centered on attacks on standalone mainframe computers or wide-scale networks. Back in the 80s and 90s, that was more of a national security concern. So it was assumed that the responsibility for solving it lay solely with the federal government, specifically the National Security Agency. That Agency is devoted to electronic security. Hence, you know where their focus would be." Lucy said, laughing, "Yeah! strictly on the nerd stuff."

The Doc smiled and added, "The problem is that the information age came along, and it's based on distributed architectures and the internet. That expanded the attack surface way past strictly electronic threats." Lucy said exasperated, "Let me stop you right here, Doc. You keep dropping terms on me that I don't understand. So, what in the world is an attack surface?"

The Doc cackled and said, "She asks the right questions." He added, "The attack surface is the sum of a given protected space's potential points of vulnerability. For instance, the common access points of a computer network are part of the electronic attack surface. The problem is that the adversary can cause as much harm or even more if they can convince the person who operates the network to hand him your data. So, there are also physical and human threats. Physical and human exploits are two new threat areas with a completely different set of assurance requirements. Meaning you have to deploy an integrated array of measures to meet each area's different demands." Lucy nodded and said, "Thank you, I understand that."

The Doc continued, "As you can see, you have to plug all of the gaps if you want to be secure. So, every potential access point has to be mitigated by an effective set of controls. Yet, that also calls out a much wider and more varied range of things you have to think about when setting up your protection scheme. Even worse, very few of those additional points of potential harm fall into the domain of electronic security."

The Doc paused for emphasis and added, "The dilemma is that much of the current generation of thought leaders still looks at the problem as if all viable threats are electronic, which by default creates a bonanza for any enterprising thief who operates in the other two areas. That's what I mean when I say that both government and business leadership is still fighting the last war. But, unfortunately, they think it's still 1992."

Both Tom and Lucy nodded. That made sense. What was the point of investing in rigorous electronic access control when a thief could just bribe the system administrator to copy what you want onto a thumb drive? The Doc continued with, "Of course, that creates a serious problem for an organization that truly wants effective cybersecurity since the knowledge that underlies those other two attack surfaces isn't traditionally considered to be relevant to cybersecurity."

Tom said, "That's right, human security issues were never mentioned in my IT security class." The Doc said, "That's a real concern because electronic security teaching doesn't realistically address the complex human motivational and psychological factors that underlie social engineering exploit. Worse, neither electronic nor human security even considers the nitty-gritty law-enforcement issues that are part of physical security. That incredible diversity of knowledge and the lack of a single complete understanding has turned the current approach to cybersecurity into a game of whack-a-mole, which I might add, we are about to lose."

Tom said pessimistically, "The Doc's right. Several of the departments on my college campus taught some parts of cybersecurity, computer science, software engineering, and information systems, to name three. But you could never get them to cooperate because they see the problem through their disciplinary lens. So, you'd have to create a completely separate discipline to get everybody to think about the problem holistically."

The Doc looked like he'd finally gotten his two charges to their personal "Eureka" moment. He said, "But you'd have to organize that new discipline around a universally recognized body of knowledge. Fortunately, three established groups are specifically designed to develop content recommendations for the various disciplines, the ACM, IEEE, and the AIS. All three publish curricular models for their respective fields. And occasionally, they come together to develop a single unified recommendation for a new body of knowledge. That is what we have here. As soon as it became clear that a new discipline was required, those societies came together into a single joint task force to formulate a unified set of curricular recommendations. It's called 'Cybersecurity Curricula 2017, or the CSEC.'"

The Doc was on a roll. He added, "The CSEC specifies a complete set of requirements for the teaching of holistic cybersecurity. Consequently, the only thing you need to do is adapt the generic CSEC recommendations to your particular situation. Best of all, those recommendations are generally applicable. Therefore, we can use them at any level of learning, which includes secondary education. The only thing you need to have is a presentation strategy."

Suddenly Tom understood why the Doc was so eager to volunteer. The older man planned to use their project as a proof of concept to demonstrate how the CSEC could be applied at the secondary level. Tom said excitedly, "So, we can count on you to help us through this project?" The Doc said, "Of course, my young friend. Since the CSEC clarifies the confusion about what to teach, the only remaining issue is the best way to teach it. That's the real challenge."

He added, "The cybersecurity practice involves a complex and diverse set of things. Given that fact that we can't pack all of that knowledge into one course, or even a single level of education, we probably need to develop a logical sequence that takes the student from the introductory level at a suitable age, up to final-mastery at the end of the process."

Lucy was beginning to see what The Doc was getting at. She was more aware of upwardly integrated teaching approaches because she had spent her entire career starting the process. But, she said, "now I can see what you're talking about. We gear our introductory strategies to mesh with what we see the students needing to know. For instance, we teach the basics of algebra in the seventh grade even though the kids don't have the abstract thinking capabilities to formulate algebraic equations. But if we introduce the concept of notation at the lower levels, they are prepared to hit the ground running in the higher grades once their abstract thinking abilities have matured."

The Doc said, "Bingo!! That's precisely what I was talking about. The problem isn't identifying what the student needs to learn. It is a fact that our current piecemeal approach isn't systematic or coordinated. Consequently, the student isn't given the knowledge in any logically effective sequence. Instead, we just drop the subject matter on them in one single homogenous blob. It's hard to make sense out of material that is that diverse."

The Doc went on with, "If you look at the scope of the CSEC recommendations, you will see that it will take time for one individual, no matter how capable, to develop a truly functional mastery of the field. This is because a complete understanding implies that all topics have been brought together into a single unified vision. But there's such a broad range of subjects required, from hard electronic areas, like component and network security, to softer ones, like human and societal security, that the teaching process isn't a trivial endeavor." The Doc added in conclusion, "So, like all of the other disciplines, mastery of the body of knowledge of cybersecurity is best achieved by a process that introduces a topic at the lowest practicable level and then increasingly builds through higher levels of detailed understanding until you reach the desired outcome."

The Doc could see that Lucy, the practical one, was about to object, and he knew why. So he quickly added, "We aren't talking about having every student progress to a Ph.D. There are obvious stop-outs along the way. For instance, the knowledge that would qualify a person to configure and run a network is appropriately delivered in a high school or community college. And it is perfectly appropriate to end your learning years at that level. That is if network operation is your goal in life."

Lucy nodded her head vigorously, placated. So the Doc added, "However there will be a few people who are dedicated to advancing the theoretical frontier of networking. They will need a lot of further study to have a sufficient level of expertise. The same is true with encryption. The operation of a public-key service requires a basic level of technical know-how. Whereas mastering the number theory that underlies the concept of an encryption process requires infinitely more schooling."

Both Tom and Lucy nodded their agreement. The Doc went on with, "At the same time, the absolute mastery of any area of endeavor starts with a set of basic building blocks at an early point in the student's education and progresses until the student's goal is reached." Tom said, "So what that means is that, besides tailoring out the actual exercises to help our students learn the CSEC concepts, we will also have to develop a logical progression that will allow us to deliver those ideas at the right time and place, from the basic knowledge that we begin with, probably in the seventh grade, all the way up to the graduation of a fully prepared student in the twelfth grade."

The Doc said, "Yes, that's correct. The real problem isn't the teaching itself, although that will also be a challenge. The real question will be how to correctly stack one concept on top of another in a phased order that will be both logically correct and suitably complete. Remember, there are eight, large, highly diverse areas in the CSEC, and in the end, they'll all have to come together in a unified vision of best practice."

Lucy said firmly, "The devil will be in the details. However, I believe that we should view our general assignment as more of a curriculum development challenge than one where we are simply identifying the content for a single course in cybersecurity."

The Doc laughed and said, "That's spot-on, Lucy. Thanks to our friends in the professional societies, we know what content we need to deliver. But the knowledge specified for something like component security is a long way from the things you have to learn to master societal security, at least in terms of the look and feel of what we're teaching. So the question is, how do we create an appropriately staged learning experience that is geared to the developing capabilities of junior high and high school students?"

Both Tom and Lucy looked at The Doc like they hoped he would finish that sentence since neither of them knew how to start the process. The Doc gave a by now familiar cackle and said, "You already told me that you build capability through a rational process. For instance, you have to master simple mathematical logic before you can introduce symbolic thinking in algebra, and you need to know symbolic logic before you can understand geometry." He added for clarification, "Of course, even to start the process at the college level, students will also need to combine symbolic notation and geometric concepts to master calculus. But the point is that you build capability over time by arraying the right set of components in stages."

Lucy said smiling, "You lost me at geometry Doc. But of course, I teach junior high kids." The Doc laughed and said, "It doesn't matter. The point is that you move up a capability ladder to full mastery of a field by building on the knowledge that you've acquired at a lower level. So, inserting the right set of elements at each step in the process is the key to success, and those have to be organized in a way that incorporates only those things you need to know to progress to the next level of proficiency."

Tom looked like a light bulb had gone on. He said, "WOW!! We could structure that progression on Bloom." Doc and Lucy glared at him like he'd just sprouted horns. So, Tom said by way of explanation, "Lucy knows what I'm talking about since Bloom is a staple in the ed-school."

Tom said, "Bloom's taxonomy is the standard method that educators use to structure the teaching of a subject from introduction to the end-product. The lowest level is *knowledge*, which requires the student to remember facts and basic ideas. For instance, the student might memorize the five components of a network. That leads to *comprehension*, which requires the student to condense the facts they've memorized into ideas, like describing how data is transferred from component to component in a network. Then the next level, *application*, requires the student to take those ideas and use them to address a real-world problem. For instance, they are identifying how an attacker can compromise a network. Finally, there's *analysis*. That requires the student to conclude causation, like determining the causes of a novel compromise and creating an appropriate set of controls?"

For a change, the Doc looked astonished. He said, "I've never heard of Bloom's Taxonomy, but it is a perfect framework for what we are planning." Lucy added, "Just as Tom said, anybody who's ever gotten a teaching certificate knows about Bloom. It's how we sequence the delivery of either a course or a curriculum. You need to scale the learning objectives to the appropriate Bloom level. For instance, in the seventh and eighth grade, the aim is to memorize and understand the terminology, whereas we work on applying those concepts to real-world problems in the ninth and tenth grade. By the eleventh and twelfth grades, we concentrate on creative ways to deal with a new or unique problem."

The Doc said, "Bravo!!! I think we've got it. So, let's plan how we're going to approach this. There are eight knowledge areas in the CSEC, and each of those is broken down into a varied number of topics. For instance, the first category of knowledge is Data Security. That area contains eight topics: Cryptography, Digital Forensics, Data Integrity and Authentication, Access Control, Secure Communication Protocols, Cryptanalysis, Data Privacy, and Information Storage Security. Each of those comprises explicit topics that are the nitty-gritty knowledge categories that you would need to master in order to be considered an expert in that category. Of course, the people who have mastered all of those topics will be graduating from college, not the ninth grade."

Both Tom and Lucy laughed. "The underlying topics detail the actual specification of what you need to know for each knowledge unit. That is what you have to learn. For instance, there are seven topics in the Data Security knowledge area. One of those is forensics. There are nine underlying elements of forensics. Each element represents something that a student would need to master to be considered knowledgeable about digital forensics. But the level of required capability varies. I'm not a teacher. But I imagine that the first level of Bloom would be satisfied if the student were able to list the major components of the forensics process. Then level two would ask them to explain those components. Level three would require them to demonstrate how each of those applies in a forensic investigation, and level four would be the ability to discuss novel applications."

Tom said, "That makes sense. So what we need to do is create a complete mapping of the eight knowledge areas of the CSEC, which would include their component topics, and the elements of each. Then all eight knowledge areas would be elaborated by memorization, summarization, application, and analysis exercises. If we do that, then we will have put together a complete and valid cybersecurity curriculum in a box." Lucy added excitedly, "And better yet that curriculum will give us the evidence that the Superintendent asked for because it is backed by the people who have been traditionally responsible for ensuring that we teach the right stuff. Okay gang! Let's start working our way through the CSEC structure. I might finally be doing something constructive!" (Website for CSEC 2017 https://cybered.acm.org/.)

# 2

# GETTING DOWN TO BUSINESS

## Data Security

The three musketeers met bright and early the next morning. Tom had his usual Granola bar, while Lucy showed up with a dozen donuts. The Doc was overjoyed. He was picking through the box, looking for the jelly-filled ones as he said, "I think we have a good strategy going forward. Suppose we align our teaching content to Bloom levels. Then, the only thing that the instructor will need to do is decide what's suitable for their student levels."

Tom and Lucy both nodded in approval. Lucy added, "No classroom teacher wants to be told how to teach, and most of us are pretty creative. So, the idea is to give us a roadmap without dictating how the individual instructor will get to the final destination; we'll come up with ideas that nobody ever thought of."

Tom, who was the idealist, said, "But we still have to base our recommendations on something we know is right. The problem with the current models is that all rely on expert opinion, which is just one person's view." The Doc was wiping the powdered sugar off his chin as he said, "Good point Tom. There's no question that the popular view of the field is shaped by various experts, who by definition have their agenda... and that's why the computer societies got involved."

The Doc added, "The role of the societies is to promote best practice in their various spheres of influence. That's been the case for over fifty years. People in computing base their actions on best practices rather than physical laws. That's because, except for hardware that is tangible, the software isn't quantifiable. Therefore, it's impossible to confirm that a concept is correct by strictly empirical means. Nevertheless, it is still possible to pool the accumulated knowledge and experience of a diverse collection of practitioners and academics

**Figure 2.1**   Doc enjoys his donuts.

to develop a consensus opinion. That's best practice. So, in effect, the CSEC represents the commonly accepted ideas of the profession, and we can be confident that it provides the most authoritative advice about the contents of the field."

Lucy said eagerly, "So, what are we waiting for? Let's get going. If I understand it right, our approach will be to condense the topics of each CSEC knowledge unit into an explanation that will be appropriate to junior and senior high school learners, as well as provide a sample of practical methods for teaching that content." The Doc was brushing donut crumbs off the front of his old v-necked sweater as he said, "Exactly! So, let's start with Data Security."

### Topic One: Why Is Data Security Important?

Good old practical Lucy asked the obvious question, "Seriously Doc, what does data security have to do with cybersecurity? I thought that the aim of cybersecurity was to protect the computer." The Doc laughed and said, "I can always count on you to ask good questions, Lucy. It's a common misconception that the role of cybersecurity is to protect the physical machine. If you think about it, the machine itself is relatively worthless compared to the data that it contains. In fact, in the early days, before we began throwing around fancy terms like cybersecurity, we used to call the field *Information* Security."

Both Tom and Lucy looked like they'd never heard that before. The Doc added, "There's no reason why you should know that? The term information security went out of vogue a decade ago." Then he turned serious, "Data is society's lifeblood. Without it, there would be no records of our transactions. People wouldn't know what they've bought or their bank balances. Businesses wouldn't be able to serve customers or make managerial decisions. So in some respects, assurance of the information that's in a computer might be the only truly legitimate purpose of cybersecurity."

He added, "The problem is that people and organizations can't tell you exactly what constitutes a data breach, let alone how to protect against it." Lucy said, "Whoa Doc, more terminology. So, what's a data breach?"

The Doc said, "The term 'data breach' describes any unauthorized access to data." Tom said, "That's hard to get your mind around, Doc. Can you give us an example?" The Doc said, "The annual cost of data breaches could reach six trillion dollars by 2024, and over the past fifteen years, the bad guys have stolen more than 11.5 billion records. Those are the real-world effects of data breaches, and those numbers ought to keep every corporate CEO up at night."

Lucy said, "Okay, I can see why data security is so important. But how in the world do we help our teachers fit something so ridiculously big-picture oriented into a classroom experience?" The Doc said, "That's why we have the CSEC recommendations. They comprise all things that a student might need to know to protect data. So, let's see what it says about it."

Tom, Lucy, and the Doc opened their copies of the CSEC and leafed through the first twenty-three pages until they reached Chapter Four of the model. That's where the recommendations for best practice began. The first section was titled "Data Security," and it contained a godawful six-page table that was divided into three columns, "Knowledge Units," "Topics," and "Curricular Guidance." Lucy sighed and then casually tossed her copy of the CSEC back over her shoulder. She said, "This is nonsense!! How in the world am

I supposed to make anything out of all of this gibberish, let alone tell somebody how to use it?!"

The Doc laughed and said, "The first time I saw the CSEC, those were my sentiments exactly. But if you look more closely, you'll see that the table comprises a hierarchy of elements starting with seven fundamental building blocks of base data security. Then it progresses through each of the topics in those blocks down to the exact things you need to know about each topic."

He added dryly, "It's the detail for those topics that are frustrating you. I'm sure that there are places where you would have to master all of those ideas. But keep in mind that we only want to make our students aware of the fundamental concepts of data security, not turn them into data security experts. All we need to teach them are the general principles and the application of each of the elements of data security."

Tom said, "In educational circles, that level of learning is called 'awareness.' So, it says here that the student has to be aware of the purpose and intent of the seven generic knowledge units of data security, *cryptography, digital forensics, access control, secure communication protocols, cryptanalysis, data privacy,* and *information storage security.* That's a confusing bag of things."

The Doc said, "If you organize that group by their purpose rather than the way it's presented in the CSEC, you will see that there are three logical operations that a computer performs on data; it either *processes, transmits, or stores* it: (1) **access control** applies to the processed part, (2) **communication protocols** applies to the transmitted part, and (3) **storage security** applies to the stored part. Then, (4) **cryptography** and (5) **cryptanalysis** are two sides of the same coin when it comes to ensuring that the information can't be read, while (6) **digital forensics** is the specialized process for investigating data breaches. Finally, (7) **privacy** is more of the desired state than an actual security activity. In many respects, privacy is just the intended outcome of the other six best practice areas."

Lucy said, "Okay, I see how those things relate. Now, we have to explain the purpose of each of them and provide some simple exercises to help the students get a general idea of how to do data security."

### The Basic Elements of Data Security: Processing, Transmitting, and Storing

The Doc said, "As I mentioned, three of the data security knowledge areas capture the essential functions of data protection. So, the *Access Control* knowledge unit, the *Secure Communication Protocols* knowledge unit, and the *Information Storage Security* knowledge unit cover the waterfront concerning basic data security. Consequently, we should consider those first." Tom said eagerly, "That makes sense, and because the primary role of a computer is to process data, access control ought to be the first area we tackle."

The Doc said, "That's right, in some respects, access control is what most people are thinking about when they use the term 'cybersecurity.' But we have to be careful about how we discuss access control since data security requires more than just regulating access to the system. We also have to ensure that there is sufficient control over threats that originate in the general environment."

Lucy said, "I can see that. But, if we only concentrate on ensuring virtual access, the bad guys would take a different approach to stealing data, like swiping laptops. So, we have to make sure that all of the physical data security requirements are covered as well. That means that students have to understand every aspect needed to ensure a safe virtual and physical environment. We even have to touch on the long-term requirements like how to dispose of data once it is no longer needed securely."

The Doc said, "That's an excellent summary, Lucy. If you look at the CSEC model, you will see that it approaches data security from both a virtual and physical perspective. The virtual approaches are what computer people traditionally call 'access control.' Those mainly comprise the technological steps that guarantee that entities seeking access to a given data resource have been properly authenticated and authorized. The authentication and authorization process is what determines each user's access rights."

Tom was looking at the specifications for access control in the CSEC. He said, "So according to this, we have to familiarize our students with the common practices in *virtual access, physical access,* and the methods for creating a *secure design.*"

Lucy was looking at the table too. She said, "According to this table, we need to start by having the students learn the basic principles for securing data." Tom said, "That seems reasonable." Lucy went on with, "There are three topics. First, the students need to be given a general idea of how they confirm their identity. The term is *authentication*. Then there are ways to ensure that the individual only has access to the information they are permitted to see. That's called *authorization*. And finally, there are the real-world security measures that are used to protect data from *physical* access."

The Doc said, "That's right, Lucy. The idea is only to give access to those who have a right to use the system. So first, the students need to learn ways to establish a unique identification basis for every entity permitted to enter the system. It's like granting a passport to each user. That way, the access control function will differentiate between legitimate and illegitimate access requests. Thus, the process for providing valid authentication credentials is the key first step in any form of access control."

Tom said, in my college class, we learned that "Identity is typically established via some form of unique token. That's generally just something a person knows – for instance, passwords, or PINs, something a person has – for example, a credit card, a magnetic room key, or a personal characteristic – for instance, fingerprints, voice, or retinal scans. This latter area is known as biometrics. Finally, there is such a thing as multi-factor authentication. You use a combination of these approaches to assure identity, for instance, a bank card and a pin number."

### EXERCISE

### AUTHENTICATION IN ONLINE SHOPPING

We tend to take the amount of trust needed to buy something online for granted. Go to Amazon.com and highlight the ways that authentication comes up when you buy something. Include third-party sales and customer reviews. Is the authentication sufficient? What would you change to make the experience more secure?

Lucy was still looking at the CSEC table. She said, "The next thing is authorization; what in the world is that?" The Doc said, "Authorization is where the principles like least privilege apply. You have to ensure that an entity's access to data is limited to only those they have a right to see, so you assign access privileges to each user based on their need to know. The machine has a record of what each individual's rights are, and so it can regulate what they can see."

Tom said, "We studied that. The privilege assignment is done via automated access control lists, which are termed 'ACLs.' ACLs are just a simple listing of authorized users and their access privileges. The ACL is consulted every time a user requests access. That process applies whether it's the machine using it to decide about user privileges, or a guard at the gate using it to decide whether the person can enter a secure space."

The Doc clapped and said, "Perfect, Tom. Two approaches to that are used in the real world. The most common is *Role-Based Access Control* or RBAC. That approach assigns access rights to an individual based on their membership in a group. The groups are typically established and managed based on the user's role in the organization. So, for instance, such roles as manager and worker, or teacher and student would all have different privileges associated with them. But every member of each of those groups would have the same rights."

The Doc added, "The other approach is called *Mandatory Access Control*, or MAC. That is a more cumbersome process because it assigns access privileges based on a classification and clearance system. Every person in a MAC structure is given a clearance level geared to their level of trustworthiness. That determines the sensitivity of the data they can access. For instance, most MACs have four layers, unclassified, sensitive, secret, and top-secret. That ensures the right amount of confidentiality, in that users cannot access data that is classified above their level of clearance. However, the process of keeping track of all of the clearances and privileges is very costly to maintain. So, it is most frequently used by the government to protect its secrets."

## EXERCISE

### ACCESS CONTROL AT HOME

Access control can be used in many places aside from large company computer systems. List three different ways in which it is used at your own home. Is it effective or ineffective? Why or why not?

The Doc said, "Of course, there are also the various methods used to control physical access to data. Physical access control involves the protection of secure physical space. We have been practicing some form of that since the Romans. But with cybersecurity, the emphasis is on protecting access to processing and data storage spaces. The simple examples of that kind of secure space are the areas containing computers or where all the data storage media is kept. That kind of protection is enabled by secure architectural design, which looks at the overall layout of the physical space and puts the appropriate barriers and checkpoints in place. The most important thing that our students need to understand is that the physical space that the information resides in has to be safeguarded as robustly as the virtual processing activities."

### EXERCISE

### PHYSICAL ACCESS CONTROL AT SCHOOL

Take a walk to the computer lab at your school. If you don't have a lab, use a computer classroom. Look around to identify the forms of physical access control that have been used to protect that room and the computer devices inside. Determine if those controls in place are adequate. Why or why not? Write a sample letter to the Superintendent making recommendations on what you would do differently to protect the room and what is inside.

Lucy said, "It seems to me that authentication, authorization, and physical security are pretty specific topics since their aspects of good access control. Hence, they would be part of a cybersecurity curriculum. But the CSEC raises the topic of secure design. How do you teach students to design an access control system? Maybe we shouldn't even consider it since that topic seems pretty abstract to me."

The Doc said, "Another good question Lucy. The crucial point to get across to your students is that access control ensures two of the generic purposes of cybersecurity – *confidentiality* and *integrity*. The third quality, '*availability*,' is a different aspect. So we'll deal with that later. But two commonsense principles underlie ensuring the first two conditions. Those always have to be captured in a design."

Tom said cautiously, "Confidentiality and integrity are pretty high-level concepts. How do we make that into something that a junior high or high school student can understand?" The Doc chuckled and said, "It's easy-peasy when you boil the whole thing down to the quality you are trying to ensure. With *confidentiality*, we want to make sure that the information can only be accessed by people who are authorized to see it. We use the authorization process, which we just discussed, to assign the individual's access privileges. But we have to design the existing access control system in such a way as to enforce that condition. We also have to make certain that people at a higher level of privilege can't share data with somebody with a lower level of privilege. For obvious reasons, that approach is called 'no-read-up.'"

Lucy said, "So the way you ensure confidentiality is to create a set of increasingly secure layers that encompass information items at a common level of privilege. Then build a system that ensures that people can only access the levels they have a right to see and no higher."

The Doc said, impressed, "Bravo Lucy, you hit the nail on the head!! But we also have to prevent data at a lower level of trustworthiness from corrupting more reliable data. That's the other side of the coin, and it's termed 'no-write-up' for obvious reasons." The Doc added, "That opposite condition preserves integrity. You ensure the integrity of the data by ensuring that data that has not been appropriately vetted is not included in your trusted files."

Tom said, "Just checking, you said, 'no-Write-up' not 'no-READ-up?'" The Doc said, "Yes, and it's vital that you understand the difference. The whole point of integrity is to protect data at a higher level of confidence from being contaminated by less reliable data. The purpose of no-write-up is to avoid mixing data that has not yet been shown to be correct with data known to be accurate. That is achieved by partitioning the valid data into secure layers based on the known level of integrity of the contents. It's the same process that we used to ensure confidentiality, but the layers' contents are decided by the data's level of trustworthiness, not clearance. Since this approach provides the accuracy of records, it is the backbone of IT activity in a business setting. The whole point is to design explicit functions that ensure no-write-up and no-read-up for every system."

Tom said, "Okay, that disposes of all of the CSEC recommendations for the virtual environment. But how are we supposed to teach students how to ensure that data doesn't fall into the wrong hands? I mean, I can see how you implement virtual controls to prevent computerized data from being harmed through misuse or even the misconduct of the people inside the organizations. That's just a matter of installing suitable automated control mechanisms. But how do you ensure against a loss or abuse from such things as deliberate theft, leaks, or simply human error?"

The Doc gave his customary manic cackle and said, "That is a much more difficult problem by far, which might explain why there are so few best practices associated with data security in the real world. But there are some common things that we need to consider at least. First and foremost, there is the simple hypothesis that 'You can't protect it if you don't know what you have.' So when you set up a physical data security function, finding out precisely what data you own is the first thing that has to happen."

The Doc said, "Unfortunately, that means you have to go through a formal process of inventorying and labeling each meaningful data asset. That process is called '*classification*' and it is not a task that most organizations want to do. But you have to know what data they possess and how it is accessed before you can put together a process to monitor and control it. Hence it's necessary."

Tom said, "I guess that's obvious; otherwise, you are just shooting in the dark. But don't you also need some kind of formal mechanism to differentiate the data you identify by its criticality. If you don't have priorities, you will be stuck trying to secure everything that isn't practical. Placing your assets in layers by their importance is the basis of the defense-in-depth concept that we talked about, right?"

The Doc said, "Absolutely! The only way to ensure reasonable control over data is to identify and classify it by its level of sensitivity. That's the first step in assigning and monitoring privileges. Then, we can set up a secure space once we know what our priorities are and monitor the flow of data into and out of that space in such a way that we can hold people accountable for its security. So, your students need to understand how to prioritize data and then distribute it into increasingly rigorous levels of protection. Once you strip it down to its basic functions, that's a sorting exercise. But it is the key to creating a true defense-in-depth scheme."

## EXERCISE

## MAKING YOUR LIST AND CHECKING IT TWICE

Create an Excel spreadsheet containing a list of the drives on your personal computer. Then for each drive, list each folder on that drive. Now list the name of each application and data file within each folder. You don't need to include the application or operating system files. What is essential is just the data files you create using the applications. Now, develop columns across the spreadsheet that categorize your files, ranking them based on: Non-Private, Personal/Private, and Top Secret. After completing the spreadsheet, describe what you learned about data identification and labeling. Given what you now know about the files on your computer, would it be easier or harder to apply access control to those files?

**Ensuring Secure Data Transmission: Secure Transmission Protocols**

Lucy, Tom, and the Doc were pretty satisfied with what they'd done with the processing aspect of data security. So, they turned their attention to data's next logical state, which is "transmitted." Lucy's sharp eye caught the apparent contradiction in the CSEC. She said, "What's the difference between secure transmission protocols, which is what we are looking at here, and network security? Doesn't the CSEC devote an entire knowledge area to data transmission? So, why are we also covering it here?"

The Doc said, "Your usual good point, Lucy. Network security is a critical topic because we live in an interconnected world. Unfortunately, many people equate cybersecurity strictly with network security. But what we are looking at in the case of data transmission protocols is a much more limited topic. Data transmission protocols are the building blocks that underpin the data transmission process; specifically, the CSEC focuses on the transmission protocols used by the World Wide Web. Those are the 'telecommunication protocol,' or TCP, and the 'internet protocol,' or IP. Those are both contained in a conceptual model of the industry's standard framework for conceptualizing a data communication system. It's called the 'open systems interconnect' model, or OSI. OSI describes the way that the various data communication elements, and specifically how the internet lets us send emails, use Facebook, and post pictures of cute kittens, all within a single seamless environment."

Tom piped up. "I remember those protocols; we studied them in my information technology program. TCP/IP is the signaling process that enables data transmission over the World Wide Web. It lets different types of devices interact with each other irrespective of their type." The Doc said, "That's right, Tom, TCP provides the transmission capability for messages, just like the postal service does for a letter, while IP is the addressing function that allows those letters to be delivered. Our students have to understand how each of those two protocols inter-operate and how they work with each other to enable the secure delivery of data. At a minimum, your students should at least be conversant with the terminology."

Tom said pleased, "That's right, Doc. There are two aspects if we want to teach it. First, students have to define the basic purpose and function of the protocols themselves; you know what I'm talking about, how TCP/IP works within the OSI model. Then to understand how those two protocols underwrite the overall process of transmitting data, the students should list the various layers in the OSI model. Consequently, we need to ask students to simply describe the TCP, its purpose, and how it operates and describe the IP and how it operates. Then they would need to list and describe the seven layers of the OSI Model and how each of them operates."

The Doc said, "Yes, Tom, that exercise might seem a little over-technical. But this is just a means of building awareness of the basic model and the transmission process. First, your students need to know that these two protocols exist and how they operate within the general framework for communicating data. Then, of course, once they move up to higher levels of education, they can begin to think about the details of packets and packet switching. But the simple understanding of what a protocol is and how they work within the overall framework is a critical security knowledge basic."

## EXERCISE

## BE GOOD AND FOLLOW THE RULES

Protocols are the "rules" that data communication must follow between one computing device and another. First, browse the internet for resources on the OSI and TCP/IP telecommunication models. Then in a word processor, create a document containing: a table with a list of the layers of the OSI model together with their definition and a table containing a list of the layers of the TCP/IP model with their definitions. Then provide a summary of how the individual layers of each model compared to the layers of the other.

Tom said, "So, we also need to provide background on network attacks and how they're countered – right?" The Doc said, "For our purposes, we only need the students to understand the two ways that networks can be attacked. Those are either passive attacks or active attacks." Lucy said, "What's the difference between the two, and what do we need the students to know?"

The Doc said approvingly, "That's the right question, Lucy, and it's a straightforward distinction. Passive attacks don't disturb the network's operation. An example of that kind of attack would be a classic 'man-in-the-middle' exploit where the intruder just sits inactively in the background and picks through the network traffic looking for interesting tidbits of information. We can have the student describe how a man-in-the-middle attack works and what harm might occur from it."

Tom said, "Seriously, how do we defend against somebody who's just sitting there without doing anything detectable?" The Doc said, "Snoopers are hard to catch because they go out of their way to make sure that you don't know that they're there. Thus, the proper defense is to encrypt any critical network traffic. For example, popular encryption protocols like Secure Sockets Layer (SSL) make it impossible for passive attackers to get anything useful out of their snooping."

Then the Doc added solemnly, "Active attacks are the real problem. An active attack aims to interfere with the normal operation of the network. Thus they are very disruptive and harmful. Active attacks fall into two categories, external and internal. An external attack is popularly termed 'hacking.' Somebody outside the network launches it. Those attacks are best addressed by the many common network protection devices such as firewalls and encryption, even defense-in-depth design. We need the students to understand what each of those protection mechanisms is and how they work to thwart external attacks."

Then he added in a cautionary tone, "Of course, there are massive external attacks such as distributed Denials of Service (DDOS), which are designed to shut down network operation on a broad scale. Those are hard to prevent. But they prevent the third critical requirement of data security which is availability. Therefore, we also need students to understand the difference between a targeted attack and one aimed at denial of service. We also need to stress the importance of having a good backup and continuity plan because of DDOSs."

The Doc stopped and added, "An internal attack is a much more serious situation because the conventional perimeter protection approaches that we rely on have already been bypassed." Lucy looked horrified. She said, "So what do we do about those!!" The Doc said, "The most common counters to active attacks are mechanisms such as automated network intrusion detection systems (NIDS) and host-based intrusion detection systems (HIDS). Those can be effective when installed and maintained properly because they are set to identify any abnormal behavior that is a trademark of an internal attack. So, the students need to know specifically how a NIDS and a HIDS operate and how they are configured and maintained."

Tom said, "So what do we need to convey to our students?" Lucy, who was an expert at boiling things down to their basics, said, "I don't know about you, Tom, but I think it's only necessary for my students to understand that there are explicit ways that networks can be attacked and be able to name some of the common types of attack and their prevention mechanisms, like firewalls and encryption. Then, when they get up to your level, they should also be able to describe those preventive mechanisms in simple applied terms, like how SSL or an automated network intrusion detection system provides protection."

Tom said, "I agree, Lucy. This is a matter of awareness again. The students should be able to see that there is a standard structure to the process by which data is communicated and that there are some very nasty things that can mess with that process. At my level, they should be able to describe the details of the most common protection mechanisms and their relevance to the overall process of data protection. For instance, they don't have to be able to install and configure a firewall. But they need to know how one operates."

## EXERCISE

### LET'S GO PHISHING

Browse the internet for websites providing information about passive and active attacks. After learning more about the two main attack categories, consider this; phishing is a type of cyberattack in which you are sent emails appearing to be an honest company, but you are dealing with a cybercriminal. Their purpose in contacting you is to try to get your personal information. Is phishing a form of passive or active attack? Explain your answer.

### Ensuring Secure Data Storage: Information Storage Security

Tom said happily, "This is beginning to make a lot more sense to me. We're giving our students the know-how to protect data in its three states, processed, transmitted, and stored. We've discussed the first two. So all we have left to discuss here are the recommendations for data-at-rest. That involves the things that you need to do to ensure that data is safely stored and then safely disposed of once it's no longer needed, right?"

The Doc said, "You're getting the hang of things, Tom. Since most modern cybersecurity thinking is aimed at the dynamic aspects of data, in essence, the processing and transmitting, a lack of attention to protecting it offline, or once it is ready to be disposed of, is one of the critical weaknesses in any cybersecurity protection plan. The problem is that massive amounts of data are always kept in storage because that data represents the organization's collective memory. Consequently, stored data is perhaps a more critical source of loss or compromise than the small amount of data that is currently in motion."

The Doc added. "Data is still valuable whether it is stored on a hard drive, laptop, flash drive, or archived in some other way, and it is something that can be easily stolen or misused via physical attacks. So, protection of data-at-rest is a serious topic." That prompted Tom to ask, "Are there ways to ensure a proper level of security for data that is being stored or disposed of?" The Doc said, "Sure, current thinking recommends encrypting stored data. But there are other considerations such as data masking and ensuring the secure erasure of data after its useful life cycle. There are even legal considerations for data storage."

Lucy said, "Explain that statement, Doc." The Doc said, "Sure, encrypting stored data and database files is the best way to hedge any risk of losing it. Encryption hardens the stored data at a relatively low cost. The encryption processes we are talking about here are the same as network encryption approaches. You typically protect all of the data in the file or database irrespective of its criticality. The requirement to encrypt stored data is mandated by local, state, and national laws and regulations. In the end, the primary consideration is the overhead cost of encrypting data versus simply storing it. So, it's a business tradeoff. That's true for both files and also databases."

## EXERCISE

### DISCOVERING BITLOCKER

On a Windows 10 or greater computer, click on the Start button and then type "encryption." Examine the BitLocker dialog box that appears. Is BitLocker turned on? There are three BitLocker administrative tasks that can be performed through that dialog. Which two should never be performed except in the event of an emergency?

Tom said, "Isn't most data kept in databases and other interactive repositories, like the cloud? It seems to me that the cost would be substantial if you tried to encrypt everything you have in those places. So there just doesn't seem to be a benefit."

The Doc said, "Spot on Tom. That's why you need to audit your stored data assets regularly. Active and systematic auditing of file and database transactions should let you spot any signs of trouble, like insider activity, or external attacks on the database. It should also help you identify any suspicious activity involving data."

Toms said, "It says here that penetration testing is important. What role does penetration testing play in data security?" The Doc chuckled and said. "You're getting good at this, Tom. Because, in the end, the best way of evaluating the security of your data is to attack it yourself. That approach is generically termed penetration testing. You can do it yourself if you have qualified white-hat hackers on staff or use third-party services specializing in penetration testing. You don't need to turn your students into hackers to teach this. All you need to do is familiarize them with the concept of white-hat hacking and discuss some of the simpler, more common methods."

Lucy said, "I don't understand this last one. Why do you need to worry about data if you erase it and what does 'masking' mean?" The Doc said, "That's perfectly understandable since both of those topics belong in a business school curriculum, not ours. But in general terms, students need to know that data does not go away if it's simply deleted. There have to be more secure ways to erase important data assets, such as special programs to overwrite the data completely. A range of products on the market will ensure that data is unrecoverable. Your students should probably just learn the concept and how one of those products works."

Lucy said, "Okay, I see that, but what about this 'masking' term? What is masking, and is that something we need to cover?" The Doc said, "Well, masking is primarily used by businesses to conceal personally identifiable information (PII). All masking involves is changing the values in sensitive items of data so that the form and structure of the items are the same, but the information itself is altered so that it's unusable. You see an example of masking most often when you are only given the last four digits of your credit card and the rest of the number is just a series of x's. You should probably explain what masking is and why it's done to your students. But that should be discussed at a higher level in the education process."

Tom said, "Okay, last but not least, we have legal issues. What does that mean, and is it something we should cover?" Lucy knew that those were. She was married to a lawyer. She said, "Think about it. The body of civil law is built around contracts, liabilities, and compliance. If you are holding somebody's data, you have a legal responsibility to protect it. That's normally spelled out in the contract that you make between the data provider and the organization responsible for securely handling it. If there is a failure to keep the data safely and reasonably, then negligence law applies, and that gets worked out in court."

The Doc added, "And besides the general obligation to protect an individual's data, there are laws and regulations on the books that spell out specific requirements for data protection. Those exist only in certain industries and in the European Union. But if you are in a regulated industry, you have to have explicit systems and processes in place that provably demonstrate that you comply with the law. If not, there are fines and even jail time."

Tom said, "But what do I cover in my classroom?" Lucy said, "I think that we need to make the student aware of what I just said, that the person holding the data is obligated to protect it, that those obligations are spelled out in a contract and that the holder might be subject to legal proceedings if they don't. We might provide some examples for that, as well as have them generally learn how a few of the major compliance laws like Sarbanes-Oxley and HIPAA work. This is not something we should dive into, it is really just a one day, or one week topic."

## EXERCISE

## PROTECTING YOUR CELL PHONE DATA

The cellphone has become a very popular device for voice and data communication. Many people don't realize how much data is put into their cell phone and transmitted everywhere around the world. Take some time to reflect about the type of data you send through your cellphone or store within it. Then research your cell phone carrier's website to see if you can locate any information about what they do through contract or as a commitment to regulations to protect the data you enter into your phone. Write a short summary about what you found.

## Making Data Indecipherable: Cryptology

The Doc said, "Okay, we've covered the basic operations on data. Now let's take a look at the ways of protecting it by making it unreadable except by authorized parties. The process that does that is called cryptology." Tom said chipper as a little bird, "Cryptology is a Greek word. It means 'hidden writing.'" The Doc said, "Yes… Cryptology modifies a message in such a way that only the person who knows how it was scrambled can unscramble it. It is a super-important function for data security because it ensures strict confidentiality and integrity of a trusted communication."

The Doc added, "The process that's used to create the hidden message is called encryption. The process for unscrambling it is called decryption." He stopped and took a bite out of his third jelly donut, chewed reflectively, and added, "Cryptology employs a very specific means. The generic term for the process is 'ciphering,' but regular folks would just call it a secret 'code.' Turning a message into a coded representation requires a shared basis for doing it, like the secret decoder ring that you found in a box of cereal. Only you and the recipient share the magic ring, so only you and that person can decipher a message."

Tom said, "I know that there have been encryption methods since the dawn of time. So let's start there. When we studied encryption in school, we learned about the various physical methods for encoding messages, such as staff ciphers and book ciphers. There were also displacement and substitution ciphers."

The Doc said, "That's right, Tom, ciphers are used to hide, or 'encipher' information. The ciphering process is reversed to translate or 'decipher' the message. Physical ciphers need a tangible object like a staff or a codebook. Those are often innocuous things, but they can also involve highly complex mechanisms like the German Enigma machine. Since we don't have access to a U-boat, where the Enigma machine was kept, we should concentrate on a few simple mechanisms like a staff cipher or a book cipher in our classrooms.

Staff ciphers probably go back to the dawn of time. We know that the Greeks, particularly the Spartans, used a scytale mechanism, which in Greek means "baton." The scytale was a cylinder of a specific diameter with a strip of parchment wound around it. The message was written along the strip of parchment and sent. The recipient simply took a baton of the same diameter, wrapped the parchment around it, and read the message." Lucy said, "That's neat, I'm sure the students would enjoy doing that."

The Doc added, "Book ciphers are like the codes you see in old spy movies where the message needs a book to decode it. The code might be something like 3-12-26, which means the coded word would be the third word on the twelfth line of page twenty-six of the book. But, of course, that would be meaningless information unless you knew which book. So there had to be an accompanying 'code book' that both parties shared. That's where that term comes from."

Tom said, "In both cases the encryption method would be pretty obvious. But the hard part would be knowing exactly which shared object it was based on. The wrong diameter staff would produce gobbledygook, using the wrong book would do the same thing. So the essence of the ciphering process was keeping the exact method of encryption secret. That's the case with every other simple ciphering approach like substitution, and transposition."

Lucy said, "Give me an example?" The Doc said, "In a substitution cipher, the letter is replaced by another one a fixed number of places down the alphabet, for instance the letter A might shift three places to C and B would become D. That is called the Caesar cipher after Julius Caesar who used it to keep his messages private. It probably worked in 44 BC, but modern approaches rely on advanced number theory to perform the substitutions."

Tom added, "The same with transposition, where the ciphering depends on something positional like the direction the message is written in. The easiest approach would be to write it out backward, where 'goodbye' would become 'eybdoog.' Leonardo da Vinci wrote his diaries that way. It was easier for him to do that because he was left-handed. But you could still read them with a mirror." Lucy laughed and said, "Those approaches wouldn't be so secret since the method is easy to guess." The Doc said, "You would think so. But modern methods like elliptic curve make it impossible to uncover the basis for the transposition."

Lucy said, "So let me get this straight because I am going to have to teach this to seventh graders. You are saying that if they know a simple substitution approach, like the Caesar cipher and a transposition method like writing a sentence backward, they will understand the basics of cryptography?" The Doc said, "When you strip the process down to its fundamentals, that's about it. They would need number theory to get to where we are currently at, but they wouldn't run into that topic until grad school."

Tom added, "Except for one very critical missing piece, which is best illustrated by the book cipher. That is the concept of keys." The Doc said, "That's right, Tom!! Book ciphers are harder to break because even though the method is easy to guess, you have to know which book was used and then have to have it handy to decipher the message. So there are two things involved in the process, the method, which is underwritten by the code that references a particular word in a particular book, and also the actual book. The same is true with modern cryptography. There's the method, or algorithm, which would be the coded word reference, but a key, or in the case of our example, the right book, is also required to 'decrypt' the message. So, the key is an essential element."

Tom said, puzzled, "Explain that!!" The Doc cackled and said, "The key is the key. See, I made a funny." Then he continued more seriously, "A key is an element that ensures the secrecy of the message. For instance, a common way to code a message is to substitute the number that denotes each letter's position in the alphabet. That's the Caesar cipher. So, C-A-T would be 3-1-20." He added, "But since substitution is a well-known way to encrypt something, people would quickly figure out that 3120 spells 'cat.' However, if you multiplied 3120 by a random number that only you and the recipient knew, like 21, you would get 65520, which doesn't spell 'cat' in any known language. Yet, if both parties in the exchange knew that 21 was the secret multiplier, the message could still be sent and read securely. That arbitrary element is what we call a 'key.'"

The Doc added, "Modern keys are very complex mathematically derived functions, not actual codebooks. But that second layer of absolute secrecy is the thing that makes modern encryption so hard to break. In modern cryptography, there are two types of keys: symmetric, or 'shared,' and asymmetric, 'or public.'"

Tom said, "I studied that. Symmetric keys are shared between the sender and the recipient. Both parties use the same key to encrypt and decrypt a message. The key itself is a complex mathematical product. So, the message will be secret as long as the shared key is only known to the sender and receiver. Therefore, most attacks on those kinds of systems aim to uncover the key. You see that all of the time in spy movies where the goal of the agent is to steal the key."

The Doc added, "Secret key systems are hard to break, which is why they are used in applications like diplomacy and the military. But it would be impossible to use a private key system in business because encrypted messages are sent between people who barely know each other. That is why the asymmetric or public key system was created. There are two keys in a public key system. The keys are generated in pairs by the same mathematical operation. The sender uses their secret key to encrypt a message. At the same time, they also use the recipient's public key to encrypt their own secret key. In effect, they also encrypt the key that they used to generate the message."

Tom looked like a light bulb had gone on over his head. He said, "I get it!! The recipient gets both the sender's encrypted message and the private key encrypted by their own public key. Then all the recipient has to do is use his linked private key to decrypt the sender's secret key and then use that key to decrypt whatever was sent. It's like using two keys to open a mailbox – yours and the senders."

Lucy said, "Whoa there, isn't all the trading of keys a bit too complicated to manage between two parties." The Doc said, "Good point Lucy! That's why a trusted third party is necessary to issue and certify the public keys that are used in this process. Those organizations provide a commercial service, and they are termed 'public key infrastructures,' or PKIs. Needless to say, the number of certification agencies has been growing as public key encryption has become the norm."

Tom said, "That's right!! All we have to do is help the students understand the simple process of scrambling a message using a common method like substation or transposition and a keying approach that allows two people who don't use the same secret key to exchange encrypted messages." The Doc said, delighted, "Well done, Tom. At its humblest, cryptology involves a coding method and a unique key. So, your students would understand how encryption works if you taught them the most common techniques for scrambling a message and then how the two keying processes turn it into a truly shared secret. Of course, there is much more to encryption at higher levels in the process. But that would create the foundation that the rest of the education process builds on."

## EXERCISE

## PLAYING WITH CRYPTOGRAPHY

Three very easy ciphers used to encrypt data are: Pig Pen, Caesar, and Simple Transposition. First, spend time browsing the internet to become more acquainted with the three forms of cryptography. Then, when you feel you've mastered the techniques, go to http://highschool.spsd.org/crypt/about.html and play the accessible version of the Discover Crypt game. How well did you do?

### Cracking the Code: Cryptanalysis

Tom said, "If you can make a message unreadable using cryptology, then why is there ever any problem with security?" The Doc said, "That's true, Tom. But the problem is that the bad guys are always trying to crack our code, and they would be able to read all of our encrypted data if they ever successfully did it. Furthermore, given encryption's role in keeping our computerized data confidential, a bad guy cracking our codes might have catastrophic effects.

In the case of cryptology, attackers use a process called 'cryptanalysis' to try to break our encryption and read our messages." Lucy said warningly, "More obscure terminology Doc." The Doc laughed and said, "Basically, a cryptanalyst aims to figure out the coding approach and the key."

Tom said, "So what do we need to teach our students? Cryptanalysis seems like a pretty dense mathematical topic." The Doc said, "It wouldn't be helpful to get into things like factoring or statistical attacks. But we should try to help our students think like an attacker. So, we have to give them an overview of the various approaches used to break encryption. If the students know a couple of the common ways that an adversary will try to attack them, then they will be generally aware of the issues that they need to consider when selecting an encryption method."

Tom, who Lucy was starting to think was a know-it-all, chimed in with, "I know of two basic strategies, brute force, and frequency analysis." The Doc smiled and said, "That's about it, Tom!! There is obviously a wide range of cryptanalytic techniques. But those two are the likeliest place to start if you want to teach this very hard-to-understand topic." He added as a note of caution, "The CSEC also mentions such approaches as side-channel attacks and attacks on public-key cryptography. But those belong in more advanced educational settings."

The doc said, "Let's try brute force attacks first. As we know, encryption involves two operations: the encryption method, which uses a key to produce a coded message, and decryption which turns the message back into something readable. But if we don't know the method or have the key, how could an attacker logically read an encrypted message? The obvious way would be to try out every possible combination of methods or keys until you find the one that works; it would be like trying every possible combination for your gym locker. That isn't a real efficient way to approach things, which is why it's called a brute-force attack. But it will work every time if you just try enough combinations."

The Doc added, "And frankly, those attacks worked pretty well until we figured out a way to counter them, which was to increase the number of potential combinations they would have to try. For instance if your combination lock has ten numbers it would take almost a thousand tries to find the right one. If the same lock had 20 numbers, it would take almost seven-thousand tries to brute force it. So the standard approach to securing a cryptologic system against brute force attacks is to increase the size of the key to a length that makes naked brute-force attacks impractical. For instance, when the fifty-six-bit Data Encryption Standard (DES) was cracked in 1999, the US simply adopted the Advanced Encryption Standard (AES), which is 128 bits."

Lucy said, "Wow, that is a really practical solution. So, what's a frequency analysis attack then?" The Doc said, "Frequency analysis just takes advantage of the fact that the written word has patterns in it. For example, it's the reason why you have to buy a vowel in Wheel of Fortune since the five vowels appear more frequently in words than 21 consonants. Thus, all the cryptanalyst has to do is look for frequently occurring patterns in the code. For instance, if the symbol # showed up at the end of a lot of three-letter words, it might be guessed that # stood for the letter 'e' as in 'the' and 'see.'"

The Doc added gleefully, "Frequency analysis might seem like a simple strategy. But it has cracked many codes in its time, including one of the most ambitious ciphers in history, the Enigma cipher. It took the British a long time, and they had to invent the proto-digital computer to do it. But they eventually broke the Enigma code using frequency analysis. Now, I'm not saying you will turn your students into cryptanalysts if you have them doing frequency analysis exercises. But it will certainly introduce them to the fundamentals of cryptography if you have them try to solve a simple sentence using both brute force and frequency analysis."

## EXERCISE

## THE FREQUENCY EFFECT

Using what you know about frequency analysis, visit the web site at the web address: https://www.dcode.fr/frequency-analysis. Type, into the "Text to Analyze" a word or phrase that you might use as a password. Then, run the analyzer by clicking on the "Launch Analyzer" button. What did the analysis tell you about the word or phrase you typed in? Next, try changing a few analysis settings and rerun the analyzer. How did your analysis change with the new settings?

### Forensics: The Investigative Aspect

Lucy said pleased, "That was productive. The next knowledge unit is Digital Forensics. I watch cop shows. I know what forensics is. It's fingerprints and such. But what is 'digital' forensics and what does it have to do with protecting data?" The Doc said, "That gets us right to the point Lucy. There are many ways that data can be harmed. But the greatest challenge of all is cybercrime."

Lucy said, "So what makes cybercrime special?" The Doc said, "Cybercrime has many subtle faces, from defrauding somebody by using a computer to stealing another person's identity or their financial information, all the way to theft of trade secrets from a business. There are also more exotic crimes, for instance, cyber-terrorism, cyber-extortion, cyber-stalking, and cyber-bullying."

Tom added smugly, "Digital forensics is a critical tool in fighting cybercrime. The problem is that there are never any physical clues in a cybercrime. That's because the internet is virtual and borderless. So, the perpetrators can commit their crimes from anywhere in the world. It's also the reason why it's so very important for our students to learn about digital forensics."

The Doc said approvingly, "You're absolutely correct, Tom. Every type of cybercrime causes tangible harm, and it is presently at epidemic proportions. But since cybercrime is virtual, our society doesn't have a real feel for how serious it is. Why the average cybercrime can be a lot more expensive than a simple bank robbery? For example, one company lost 2.7 million records to an internet exploit. At the low end, that breach cost them $238.7 million. And that loss didn't even include the collateral costs like legal fees, lost employee productivity, regulatory fines, customer losses, stock losses, and the nebulous price of bad publicity."

Lucy said, "Okay, I see why digital forensics is important. But how does it differ from regular forensics? They both look like ways to investigate crime." The Doc laughed and said, "Spot on Lucy!! In many ways there is no difference whatsoever between the purposes of classic forensics and those of digital forensics. Except, cybercrime involves virtual evidence, so the acquisition and preservation techniques for the data are different. Conventional police aren't trained in computer investigation. So, they have no knowledge of the specialized computer forensics practices that are used to collect virtual evidence. However, because the results of any criminal proceeding will eventually end up in a court of law, virtual data collection techniques also have to adhere to the same rules of evidence as to any other type of criminal proceeding."

The light bulb went on in Lucy's head. She said, "If digital forensics has to follow the same classic rules of evidence, we need to make our students familiar with the common processes for gathering and analyzing virtual data." Tom added eagerly, "But we also need to make our students aware of the universal requirements like the forensic chain of custody and analytic and authentication techniques for virtual evidence. It seems to me that the legal issues are critical. Isn't that right, Doc?"

The Doc said, "That's right, Tom. In concept, digital evidence is the same as any other evidence in that it is used to establish the causality of a crime. But the problem is that the process for collection and authentication, the chain of custody, and analysis that applies to physical evidence doesn't quite fit virtual evidence. Virtual evidence is intangible by definition. So, the assurance of correctness and authenticity is hard to establish. That's why specialized digital tools are used to support both hardware and software forensic investigations. For instance, there are digital tools that can be used to support the forensic identification and recovery of systems, or network files and saved files in a computer, or even data on mobile devices such as USBs."

Lucy was really getting the hang of things. She said, "But using those tools is out of the realm of high school and middle school study, right? Still, the basic process for acquiring and preserving evidence can be studied and applied by secondary school students, and they can use some of the basic tools."

The Doc said, "That's right, Lucy!! For instance, the logs and records that the computer generates are rich sources of forensic data and they can be easily accessed and read by even middle school students. Items such as system log files, network log files, and the files that are created and stored by end-users on the computer or on external devices such as thumb drives, or memory cards, can be identified, retrieved, and the pertinent data extracted using some basic software applications like WireShark and EnCase."

Tom said, "That would give the student the basic forensic mindset. And the teacher can even create a moot court situation where the students present the evidence and the proof of assurance that the chain of custody has been preserved." The Doc said, "Duplicating an actual court situation might be a bridge too far. But I see three knowledge factors that have to be covered in any presentation of this topic. The first thing would be the common methods for *authenticating evidence*. Authentication is the critical factor here, because it must be proven beyond a shadow of doubt that forensic evidence that is gathered as part of an investigative process is complete and correct and has not been tampered with. This is done by means of detailed and explicit *labeling* and *safeguarding* procedures at the scene, or in the forensics laboratory. It also includes documenting assurance of *safe storage*, which is normally enabled by some form of logging of the evidence. In addition, there may be some form of periodic audit held to confirm that the integrity of the virtual evidence has been preserved."

Lucy said, "Audits aren't something we could do in a seventh-grade classroom. But we could teach the students how to identify, sort, and explicitly label individual types of items from a pile of disaggregated things. We could even have them develop a way to securely store them over a period of time. It could actually be a fun week long exercise that we could do in teams, especially if there is a reward at the end for the team that can prove that what they have collected and are keeping is the most accurate representation of the problem," Tom added enthusiastically, "We can take that to the next level with my students. We can do the same thing but work with files and logs system logs."

### Privacy: Ensuring Personal Data

Lucy was looking at the CSEC. She said, "So according to this, privacy is the last unit in the data security area, and I don't understand how it fits with the rest. As far as I can tell, privacy is a state, or a condition, not something that you do to protect data, like encryption, or forensics." The Doc said, "That's absolutely correct Lucy. Privacy is a desired state. It merely implies that data in your care is confidential which also happens to be one of the three primary goals of the cybersecurity process."

Tom said thoughtfully, "In that case, doesn't privacy protection involve ensuring confidentiality of every individual's personal information, such as credit card numbers, or social security number, even something as innocuous as their address, right?"

The Doc said, "That's right Tom, and it is an absolute necessity in modern life because the theft of personally identifiable information can wreck all sorts of havoc. For instance, up to nine million people a year suffer from identity theft and the resulting legal consequences are very painful both for the individual and also for the corporation who lost the information."

Lucy said, "So what are the steps for protecting individual information?" The Doc said, "There are a wide range of approaches to mitigate the potential risk to privacy. That includes human behavioral, physical, and organizational protection measures and electronic ones. So we need to help our students understand what privacy is and its risks and give them a set of practical steps for keeping data private. But first and foremost, we need to make them understand that they have equal responsibility for ensuring their privacy."

I see three important factors that should be stressed. First, there is the need to reinforce their awareness of their responsibilities for preserving their privacy. They also need to be aware of the common threats to personally identifiable information, such as insecure posting on social media sites and phishing scams. Finally, they need to be fully briefed on the need for personal cyber hygiene. Lucy said, "That sounds more like a simple instruction process to me. We make a list of the relevant points that illustrate those topics and present them in a unit on privacy protection." Tom said, "And once they get to my level, we can look at some of the privacy laws and regulations that affect them, such as FERPA and HIPAA. That should adequately cover the essentials of the topic."

## EXERCISE

### DATA PRIVACY AT SCHOOL

All student data is protected by a regulation called the Family Educational Rights and Privacy Act of 1974 (FERPA). First, browse the internet for information about FERPA, then provide a summary about why this regulation is important to a school, a student, and a student's family.

The Doc said, "That completes the topics our students have to understand to master the concepts of data security." With that, he glanced out the window at the lengthening shadows and said, "This was a productive day's work. Let's start bright and early tomorrow with the next section in the CSEC, Software Security." With that, he stood up and brushed the crumbs of breakfast and dinner off him. They landed on Lucy's floor, and she gave him an angry look, which he completely ignored as he ambled out the door. Tom looked at Lucy and said, "Okay – he's eccentric. But that's a small price to pay for how far down the road he's advanced us." Then he rose and hiked out to his car, leaving Lucy to grab the broom and dustpan.

# 3

# SOFTWARE SECURITY

## Software Underlies Everything

The next morning, the Doc's first question was, "Where're the donuts?" Lucy said, "Until you learn to clean up after yourself, you aren't getting any donuts." The Doc grumbled, "How can we expect to get anything done if we're starving." Tom said helpfully, "I have an extra Granola bar." The Doc said crossly, "I don't eat compressed bird-seed." Lucy said, "I'll get us a box if you promise to be more careful." The Doc said eagerly, "I promise, and while you're gone, Tom and I can start developing the justification for software security."

As Lucy left, Tom said, "I know that software is important, and I know that it's a source of vulnerability, but I've never quite understood how it fits into the cybersecurity realm. You know what I mean, Doc. I can see why attacks on data have to be addressed. But how does programming fit with the concept of information protection?" The Doc laughed and said, "That's perfectly understandable, Tom, since a lot of people didn't make that connection. It's because much of the early information protection thinking concentrated on data transmission and encryption. The idea of being attacked through a defect in the underlying code was seen as another matter entirely, more in the realm of quality assurance rather than security."

Tom said, "Explain that. How could they be viewed as separate?" The Doc smiled and said, "We just didn't think about it much in the beginning. Of course, everybody knew that the two were related. But nobody ever made the formal connection. It wasn't until the NICE initiative in 2010 that software security was officially designated as an aspect of cybersecurity. And I might add that it was about time that we got software security on the same page with all the other things in cybersecurity since software underlies everything that we do in our modern world."

DOI: 10.1201/9781003187172-3

**Figure 3.1**   Doc complains about granola bars!

Tom said, "I get that. I know that the virtual universe is entirely built on software. So our students need to understand that security concerns associated with software affect all of the areas of our life." The Doc said, "That's correct, Tom, bugs and defects in software systems are how the bad guys access information or install malicious code. Attacks on our basic infrastructure, which are mainly software-driven, are hazardous because our whole way-of-life depends on virtual technology."

Tom said, "So what exactly IS software security? What's involved?" The Doc said, "In practice, software security is a process, not a particular set of actions. The measures you take to ensure security is borrowed from the disciple of Software Engineering. The software engineering body of knowledge specifies the explicit concepts, methods, and procedures you need to produce defect-free code. The necessity of eliminating defects in code is a requirement that far predates modern security thinking. So, the relevant elements of software engineering knowledge have been around in official terms for at least fifty years and formalized as a body of knowledge for at least thirty. So, there is very little that we do to assure code that isn't just simple software engineering."

Toms said, "So if the entire body of knowledge is called 'software engineering,' then why do we need an area called 'software security.'"

The Doc laughed and said, "It is a bit confusing, isn't it? Software security focuses on one specific aspect of the problem than it is an actual set of practices, although there are some additional security-oriented techniques. The fact is that what we call software assurance exists because we have to address the adversary specifically."

The Doc paused there and added, "That's the critical difference. The presence of the adversary changes everything. We didn't have to write code with attacks in mind until recently. Now we have to do that. So, we adapted the already mature set of software engineering best practices to a new task: defending the organization against an increasingly sophisticated array of attacks. But since most of the existing mitigations still rest on good programming practice, the factors that differentiate software security actions from software engineering actions are embodied in nothing more than a well-defined set of criteria that guide best practice for every software development project."

Tom said, "Let me get this straight. You're telling me that software security is just another set of specialized criteria that you use to make sure that the software is also attack-proof." The Doc laughed and said, "Strictly speaking, that's true. Software security appears to be a different field because vulnerability mitigation requires us to apply normal assurance processes like tests, reviews, and audits for a different purpose in detecting exploitable vulnerabilities. But at their core, those techniques are just the same validation and verification concepts that have been a staple of software assurance over the past thirty-five years. The additional software security criteria specify the specific assurance practices that we have to put in place to ensure against all reasonable forms of attack. In some respects, that makes software security more a planning discipline than a technical one."

Tom said, "Wow!! That's nowhere near how I viewed it. But I also didn't realize that software quality assurance and software security assurance were essentially the same with a different goal in mind. Can you give me an example?" The Doc said, "Well, for example, the organization defines the requisite level of code integrity and then deploys a specific set of tests and reviews to make certain that the specified requirements for defect prevention and modularity have been met. Of course, the best practice tests and reviews that they might use will vary as the threat picture changes. But the criteria for the level of code integrity won't. So, we aim to help our students understand that software security is a set of situationally imposed criteria that spell out the levels of integrity in unambiguous terms that must be met. Meanwhile, the actual actions that are taken to ensure that integrity, such as reviews, tests, and audits, even documentation and sustainment activities, are a constantly evolving array of routine software engineering best practices that we might use to make sure that those criteria are satisfied."

Lucy returned at that point carrying a big box of donuts. The Doc fished around in the box and selected a couple of custard eclairs. He took a bite out of the first, sat for a moment savoring the gooey taste, and said, "Because software security is established by policy, the CSEC Software Security Knowledge Area focuses on the considerations you have to keep in mind to protect software throughout its lifecycle. Hence, the concepts and principles for software security can best be understood by looking at their application at each stage of the Waterfall."

Lucy said, "Terminology Doc, what does a waterfall have to do with software?" The Doc laughed and said, "Thanks, Lucy. The Waterfall isn't a landscape feature. It's a basic lifecycle model

**Figure 3.2**   Doc explains the software waterfall.

that guides how software is created. It's been in use since 1970 to describe the development process. It involves five basic stages; specify the requirements, design the artifact, code it, *test* it, and accept/use it. So each of the CSEC software security knowledge areas introduces the fundamental security principles for that stage of the Waterfall. Then it ends with a couple of ancillary considerations, documentation, and ethics. Thus, the seven knowledge units for software security are (1) **Fundamental Principles** – e.g., the basic concepts that underlie secure software, (2) **Design** – which entails just those principles of conceptualization and architecture that apply to security, (3) **Implementation** – which covers the technical principles of programming and integration as they apply to secure code, (4) **Analysis and Testing** – these are the standard methods and models that should be associated with software testing and assurance, (5) **Deployment and Maintenance** – which are the security-focused principles for program acceptance and long-term sustainment, (6) **Documentation** – which focuses on the best practices for making software understandable, and finally (7) **Ethics** – which covers the big-picture principles that underwrite the proper operation of the software."

Lucy said, "Those all sound complicated, Doc. How do we teach seventh graders about technical stuff like software testing or even software maintenance?" Tom answered Lucy instead of the Doc, which surprised both of them. He said, "Remember, our goal is awareness. We don't need to teach the students how to perform stress tests. We just need to get them to understand the order and logic of the Waterfall process and why something you built has to be proven at each stage. The students need to understand the function of each of these lifecycle stages and the steps they have to take to ensure security. The generic principles in each of those stages can be learned and applied without asking our students to dive down into the technical details."

The Doc laughed and said, "Good summary Tom and it's true, the very last thing we want to do is bury a student in the multitude of details of the process. We just need them to see how each stage in the Waterfall relates to the others and what you need to get as a security outcome from each stage. So, that's why we should take this one waterfall stage at a time."

Topic One: Fundamental Principles of Software Security

They all looked at the CSEC and saw that the first topic was "Fundamental Principles." It was evident from the title that these would be the underlying concepts that would help guide software developers in building more secure code. The Doc said, "Many of the concepts in this section come from the work of Jerome Saltzer and Michael Schroeder, who were the first people to develop a set of high-level principles for designing and implementing secure software systems. That was in 1974, by the way, which far predates our current focus on secure coding. Those principles mostly dictate how to build security into software. They are generic in that they are platform and language agnostic. Software developers, whether they are developing new software, performing maintenance, or assessing existing software, apply these principles as a guide for making their software more secure."

Lucy said, "The CSEC lists 14 areas of discussion." The Doc said, "These are mostly high-level Saltzer and Schroeder ideas that represent the generic things a software developer needs to think about when they create their product. For example, concepts like least privilege, which dictates need-to-know and complete mediation, require the software to validate every input and provide best practice advice about designing and coding a secure product. In essence, the principles in this knowledge unit can and should be used to define an explicit set of policies, standards, and guidelines for any given software development process."

Lucy said, "There is no way a seventh-grader is going to understand the least privilege." Tom said, "But they WILL understand that you might want to tell only your best friend a secret that none of the other friends need to know. Something as abstract and opaque as 'fail-safe defaults' can be translated into 'better safe than sorry' exercises. At my level, we can even discuss what those principles underwrite in terms of protection."

Lucy took another look at the list and said admiringly, "You know you're right, Tom. If we view this as simple, common-sense advice, we can create a basic exercise for every one of these principles. So, you are saying that we should ensure our students know what those 14 principles are in terms of their basic definition and purpose. Then, as they move up the ladder to your level, we have to help them see where they apply in creating a security program. I think we can do that easily enough."

## EXERCISE

## BUILDING CLICHÉS FROM SOFTWARE SECURITY

A cliché is a catchy way of saying something. For example, the phrase "Birds of a feather flock together" is a way of saying that people with similar interests tend to become friends and gather in the same places. So take what you know about software security fundamental principles and create a cliché for each.

### Thinking about Security in Design

The Doc said, "The principles describe the overall framework for thinking about software security." Then he chuckled and said, "But we are going to have to go over the Waterfall for the rest of this area. See – I made another funny." Lucy got a "give me a break" look and said, "Based on what you said, the first two stages, specification and design, are like the place where the builder works with the customer to decide what they want their new house to look like, right? But, those two activities seem pretty nebulous to me. So, what am I supposed to get a seventh-grader to understand about design?"

The Doc said, "That is a great analogy, Lucy. It isn't hard to get your mind around the specification and design stages if you see them as the point in the process where the blueprint gets drawn up. The design itself is a difficult subject to teach in college because it is, by definition, abstract thinking. However, the security considerations are the items we need to concentrate on here, not the details of modeling and representation. So, the thing that is crucial to get across from the standpoint of the body of knowledge is that requirements and design go hand-in-hand. Meaning explicit security features have to be identified and then embedded in the design initially. More importantly, this is done independently of developing any functional requirements. So, although the title is 'Design,' the actual topic should be 'Deciding what type of security and how much security you want to have.'"

Tom said, "To implement any kind of security, we need to know precisely what weaknesses you plan to address and the explicit set of protective measures you plan to develop." The Doc said, "That's right, Tom. So, the ideas we have to get across involve implementing reasonable protection. So, the first step is to decide how secure you want to make the software. That involves identifying the specific vulnerabilities you want to address, like coding defects or logical errors. But it also requires that you characterize the environment in which the software operates. For instance, the same set of security requirements will be implemented differently if the software is meant to operate in your family home rather than outer space."

That made sense. Both Tom and Lucy nodded. The Doc continued with, "Once the protection requirements are characterized, the next two stages are the actual design activity. First, you describe all the security requirements' types and purpose, focusing only on desired protection behaviors, not functionality. Then you define the specific actions that the software must perform to achieve the desired level of protection. You also specify the development process activities that must occur to ensure that those requirements are embedded in the life cycle. Then finally, since programming is always needed to implement any given set of requirements, a definitive decision has to be made regarding the programming language that will be employed given the security requirements of that particular product. That decision is necessary because you have to match the strengths and weaknesses of a language to the specific security situation."

Lucy said, "Let me get this straight, Doc. You tell me that software design is no different from what you'd do to design a house. First, you have to make clear choices about what you want. Then you draw up a blueprint that will tell the builders what to build. And finally, you have to choose a builder with the right tools and capabilities to build the house properly. When you take out all the big words, that's just common sense."

Tom said, "You're suitable as usual, Lucy. We can probably teach this by putting the students in teams and telling them to identify the hazards for a scenario that we cook up, like, posting on Facebook and describing how they would mitigate those problems. We can even make it a competition, where the team that identifies the most threats and provides the most practical solution wins. Of course, programming languages are something we cover in the eleventh and twelfth grade. But if the students learn to identify potential environmental risks and then describe those dangers in understandable terms, I can teach them how to evaluate the strengths and weaknesses of the languages later on."

## EXERCISE

## A PARENT/TEACHER PORTAL ON YOUR SCHOOL WEBSITE

You have been asked to provide a secure parent/teacher portal design for your school website. If your school already has a portal, you have been asked to redesign what already exists to make it more secure. The portal should allow your parents to look up your class schedule, see homework assignments, get a current record of your grades, and will enable them to communicate with your teachers. Specifically, identify what security measures need to be in place to reduce or eliminate vulnerabilities within the portal.

### Building the Software Securely

Tom said, "Speaking of programming, doesn't that phase just involve what the profession calls coding?" The Doc said, "That's correct, Tom. But the body of knowledge has nothing to do with teaching students how to program. Instead, the topics presented in secure coding focus on helping the students understand how to *think securely* when doing programming work."

The Doc added, "There are six logical topics involved in secure programming, all of which have something to do with eliminating the coding errors that cause security faults. Some of them are the obvious things, like ensuring that all of the data that passes into or out of a running program is verified correctly. That's enabled by confirming that all of the places where data passes back and forth have been written correctly and that those interfaces implement the security features specified in the design. So those are the fundamental concepts that we need to concentrate on at our level."

Tom, who considered himself a programming whiz added enthusiastically, "There are more advanced considerations like error handling, which is easy enough for me to cover at the high school level. That topic simply ensures that any unanticipated or undesirable input or processing steps are identified and halted until a decision is made. We called that 'error trapping' in my programming classes, and it involves creating a shortlist of acceptable input and processing steps. After that, anything else is stopped." The Doc said, "Perfect Tom, and of course, there are also requirements in the CSEC for robust programming and encapsulation. But those belong later in the educational process, not in high school."

Lucy said, "Well, I can see where I could get my seventh graders to understand simple inputting and outputting and why the relationship between those two things must be correct and predictable. Ensuring predictable outputs is just the scientific method we teach even earlier, in grade school. I'm also pretty sure that I can get them to understand the concept of interfacing by having them play the old game of passing along a message in a chain from person to person. I might even be able to teach error checking by having one of the students hold a copy of what's supposed to be passed and make them then stop and correct the process if the message gets messed up. But it's up to Tom to teach them the essential programming techniques to check for all of that." Tom said, "That's very easy. I can teach anybody how to implement something in a language as long as we know in advance what has to happen."

## EXERCISE

## THE INS AND OUTS OF SECURE CODING

Many people don't realize that a user sitting at the computer is not the only source of input and destination of output for software. So, first, try to identify other sources of input and output. Next, see if you can list what would be required of the software that uses those input and output sources to make it less vulnerable to attack.

### Assuring the Security of the Software

Lucy said, "This has all been new territory for me. But testing is something that I'd expected to find in a software security section. In my mind, anything created should go through a series of tests to confirm that it's built correctly. But didn't you just say that we have been doing the same types of tests and reviews on software for the past thirty-five years? So where does the security come in?" The Doc said, "That is correct, Lucy. Where the difference lies is in the focus on protection rather than simple quality control."

He said, "Because we are now facing an adversary, we need to think about how to apply common testing best practices and technologies in assessing the security of the code, not just its functional capabilities. There are two ways to do this, and again, the actual techniques go back fifty years. Those are static testing and dynamic testing."

Lucy said warningly, "A lot of opaque terminologies. So what are those two things, and what's the difference?" The Doc laughed and said. "Static testing simply entails the arduous process of proofreading the code to try to spot any flaws. Dynamic testing is what most of us understand as testing. That's where we put the software through its paces, trying to identify any possible compromises. The other thing that our students need to understand is that static and dynamic tests can be done at virtually any stage after coding is complete, from the unit level to subsystem up to the system and application level."

Tom said, "If I understand it correctly, static testing is done by a human who simply reads the code." The Doc said "That's right, Tom! Static testing typically occurs early in the process, often just as the code is written. That is the case because the time it would take to read all of the lines of code in a finished system would take too long. That's why static tests are typically referred to as code reviews. Then, dynamic testing takes place at the subsystem and integration stages. In essence, once the correctness of the code has been verified. These additional tests are geared toward confirming the performance of the finished products at the unit, integration, and system level. So, there are four relevant topics in the Analysis and Testing knowledge unit: (1) **Static and dynamic testing processes**, (2) **Unit testing**, (3) **Integration testing**, and (4) **Software testing**."

Lucy said, delighted, "Based on what you just said, Doc, I can see the progression of those topics. First, you need the students to understand exactly what the purposes of static testing and dynamic testing are, and then you need to show them how those two differ in their focus and execution. Finally, the student needs to understand their role in the software development process. We even do some of that with our Raspberry Pis. I make the students write out the Python code before they input it, and I even make them run the program and report the results of what they'd just written."

The Doc said, "Wonderful Lucy, you already have the process down. Static testing is proofreading the program code to ensure that it is logical and correctly written and implements best practices. All you would have to do is add some simple security criteria that the students would have to confirm, such as proper logic and syntax, and you would have captured the purpose and intent of static testing. The performance part would involve them writing some simple security test cases. They would confirm that the program embodies error traps to prevent spurious data from entering. That is called an 'abuse case' in professional circles. The only difference between students at your level and those at Tom's would be the degree and sophistication of the programs being analyzed."

Tom said, "Yes, that's right. They are proficient in Python by the time they get to the twelfth grade, and they also know C++. The only difference is that our programs are much larger." The Doc said, "That is the reason for the next three topics. As you know, Tom, larger and more sophisticated programs are constructed in modules in what looks like a tree. We break the entire set of requirements into increasingly smaller disaggregated components. The end product resembles the basketball brackets for March Madness. Those components are then assembled bottom-up into progressively fewer and larger program objects, just like the number of teams gets smaller as the tournament progresses. Then there's eventually one winner at the top, and that is the functioning program."

Tom said, "I see that. You're saying that the software starts as many logically related pieces assembled in stages into successively larger parts. Eventually, that process produces a single integrated set of components that is the final product." The Doc said, "That's the process exactly, Tom. Because every part should be rigorously tested at the lowest reasonable point, most of the testing above the unit level, which is what that programming stage is called, is done strictly to ensure that the integration of the components is proper and carried out as planned. That is probably something you would talk about at your level, not Lucy's. Still, static and dynamic testing exercises can confirm that the parts were assembled correctly in a tiered fashion, subcomponent to a component to the system. That is what the CSEC recommends."

Tom said, "I can see how that works. We would have programming teams, and they would perform a series of analyses as the software is being built from its components exactly like a big Lego castle would be built. First, you'd test to make sure the walls were properly constructed, and then you would test to make sure that they were properly combined into towers and buildings and eventually the entire castle." The Doc said pleased, "I couldn't have said it better, Tom!"

## EXERCISE

## DEBUGGING FOR SECURITY SAKE

Static testing is the process of carefully reviewing the application source code to ensure that all possible vulnerabilities have been eliminated. Once you perform the analysis, how should you use the results? How will you determine what actions you need to make in each application area to further security measures?

### Secure Deployment and Maintenance

The Doc said, "But testing isn't the end of the road. Nobody would invest a lot of money into building a software system and never use it. So perhaps the most important part of the process comes after the thing is built. That final stage is usually termed software operations and maintenance, and it amounts to eighty-to-ninety percent of the entire time of the software lifecycle. Thus any software security curricula need to include the critical assurance aspects involved in deploying, operating, and maintaining the software in the real world."

Lucy said, "More words. What's the difference between those three?" The Doc said, "Good point, as usual, Lucy. Deployment makes sure that the software is correctly embedded within existing software systems. Nothing ever operates in a vacuum in a computer, even on your home PC. So any new program must be installed in a way that assures that it interacts properly with all of the other software on your machine. Ensuring the interactions and interdependencies between programs might not seem important. But hackers love to exploit operational gaps."

The Doc paused and added, "Sustaining the software over time is a security topic in and of itself. Operations and maintenance are normally termed 'sustainment.' But they are two different functions. Operations make sure that the system is operating as intended. In contrast, maintenance is responsible for the upkeep and repairs that are a fact of life in working a modern computer system. So, in essence, deployment is a short, practical, transitory phase in the life cycle. Whereas operational use and maintenance tasks have long-term implications for the overall security of the system."

Tom said, "How do we teach something that is so long-term and business-oriented? I mean, there must be a million activities associated with operations and maintenance." The Doc laughed and said, "There are, but that isn't the point. All three of these activities are tied to the unique situation. You can't teach the specific things you need to do in each case. But fortunately, the overall process has been condensed and documented as a set of standard practices. If the student understands the requirements of each of those practices, they can apply the specific tools they need to address a particular problem. It's like car repair. So many things can go wrong, but the diagnosis and repair are pretty straightforward and standard."

The Doc added, "All three of these generic processes are based on a set of common best practices for installation and sustainment. Most of these are aspects of knowing what you are working with, back to the car analogy. There will be a different set of requirements if there is a V8 under the hood versus a V4. So, you have to know what you've got before you start maintaining it. Then you can select the right tools and perform the proper maintenance activities. The same is true with installation and sustainment. Hence, the process always starts with a thorough examination and characterization of the existing artifact."

Lucy said, "But what does that have to do with software security?" The Doc said, "Well, the only real goal of any sustainment effort is to ensure that the software is properly and securely deployed and maintained in its environment. Essentially, this means that the assurance aspects all focus on operating and maintaining the product 'as built.' That assurance is more of a record-keeping and oversight process than anything technical. You have to use the blueprint you drew up in the design phase as the benchmark for determining whether the software continues to satisfy those requirements. If not, then adjustments have to be made to ensure that you carried out the evolution in a rational way that satisfied the original intent."

Lucy still looked confused. The Doc said kindly, "Simply put, because sustainment is an ongoing organizational function, it requires policies and a strategy to manage its day-to-day execution. The strategy ensures that the software continues to adhere to the terms, conditions, and criteria set up to ensure its secure operation. Since changes will inevitably be required, the main purpose of the software maintenance process is to make certain that whatever is requested in the way of a modification to the original product continues to satisfy the baseline configuration requirements of the original build."

Tom said, "So what you're saying is that these three stages are just some form of planning, control, and assurance activity that manages the real-world evolution of the software in such a way that the product continues to retain the security and quality that was originally specified for it." The Doc said, "Right again, Tom! Students need to be aware of the fundamentals of secure software configuration management. There are five logical elements in the CSEC: (1) **securely configuring and patching the software**, (2) **keeping the software aligned adequately with its environment**, (3) **securely operating the software within that environment**, and (4) **decommissioning/ retiring it**."

Lucy said, "Those are nerdy concepts Doc. How in the world do we teach something like configuring or patching?" The Doc said, "You don't. Instead, you concentrate on the steps you would need to take to maintain the desired integrity of the existing build. For instance, back to Tom's Lego analogy, you could have an intricate Lego structure that you would expect the students to maintain exactly as it was built, with the same features, walls, towers, battlements. Then you could tell them to make a series of changes to all of those structures but that anything they do while changing it would have to be carefully recorded, along with what was changed. Then they must justify the change in terms of how it preserves the original intent of the structures as it was first designed and built. If you ran that exercise over a semester, the students would very quickly master all of the analysis, planning, verification, and documentation features required to do secure sustainment."

## EXERCISE

## CONFIGURATION MANAGEMENT AT HOME

We often hear of configuration management when talking to software geeks. However, the same principles can and should be used to upkeep the home where you live. Have a conversation with your parents. Ask them how they assess the maintenance that needs to be performed to your home. Are repairs made to provide "quick fixes"? Or, is the goal to provide a long-term solution? Is maintenance done according to a schedule? What type of records are kept relating to the maintenance that is performed? Write a short summary of what you learned and how it would relate to what is done to secure software during the operations and maintenance phases of the software life cycle.

### Ensuring Proper Documentation

Lucy said, pleased, "That's an excellent idea, Doc. We'll make a junior high school teacher out of your yet." The Doc laughed self-effacingly and said, "I'm not tough enough." Then he added, "But you can probably see why documentation is the next item on the CSEC's list of topics for this area. Most of the life cycle involves formal plans, specifications, code artifacts, test results, and the paperwork involved in acceptance and sustainment. All of those things are part of the documentation that must be managed if you want to maintain a secure software configuration.

For example, the major byproduct of the project management phase is the project management plan which provides direction for all of the managed aspects of the project. In the software analysis phase, a requirements specification is written to define the functional and security requirements of the software. The software specification is, in turn, used during the design phase, which is guided by a design specification that dictates how the product is to be built. The software quality assurance and the security assurance plan are also created in that early phase. So, the software test plan, maintenance plan, and even the actual source code for the software artifact are documentation items. These all have to be preserved if the software's security and integrity is to be maintained over time."

Toms said jokingly, "That kind of heavy documentation might have been required back in the Pleistocene Doc. But with modern agile methods, we don't do much documentation. We just deliver the product faster-cheaper-better." The Doc said, "That may well be Tom. But without documentation, you don't have a record of what you've done, which makes it far too easy for mistakes to propagate or even outright malicious things to slip through the net. So, security and quality are sacrificed on the altar of instant gratification and corporate greed. The CSEC recognizes the implications of a lack of documentation, especially within the later phases of the software lifecycle. That's why it devotes an entire topic area to the importance of writing things down and keeping track of them throughout the process. There are four simple components in this highly practical knowledge unit: (1) **installation documents**, (2) **user guides and manuals**, (3) **assurance documentation**, and the essential (4) **security documentation**."

Tom said, "These are all some form of the user manual, right?" The Doc said, "You could see it that way. We said earlier that nothing ever functions in a vacuum in the software universe. Thus, the installation documents must be made as clear as possible because they serve as a reference point for all the changes. They ensure that the overall system is managed and evolved rationally and securely. Otherwise, you get what the trade calls 'spaghetti code' and the inevitable security gaps that entails." Lucy said, "So we just need to train our students to log their actions when they perform a change on their system, like add a new program or change its features?" The Doc said, "You couldn't have described the point of the installation documentation process any better, Lucy." Lucy said, "I assume what I just said also applies to the user manuals for each software item – right? I could see where you would make a lot of mistakes if you weren't familiar with how to operate the system." The Doc said, "There have been some estimates that up to ninety percent of all security violations are due to user error. So, you couldn't be more correct, Lucy. You have to get the students to understand how to maintain their documentation in some orderly filing system so that they can easily access the fine print advice when they need it."

Tom said, "I guess I can see where that also applies to the assurance and the security documents. You obviously can't operate a system securely if you don't have all the security advice handy. Also, the assurance documentation lets you know where the pitfalls and advantages of the product are. So, I know that you ought to be able to refer to that whenever you have a question." The Doc said happily, "You two have the hang of this area. It's just common sense, you know, to keep all of the things you might need carefully at hand, and that is all this humble little area requires. Teaching good security practice in day-to-day operation tends to get missed when dealing with exotic topics like testing and assurance. But in many instances, it is the simple understanding of the product that is more important than knowing about any of the more glamorous features. You can teach that at both of your levels by simply helping the students to understand why continuous cyber hygiene discipline is important."

## EXERCISE

## PRACTICE GOOD HYGIENE

Cyber hygiene is perhaps one of the most fundamentally essential practices any software user must be aware of and perform daily. First, watch the video "What is Cyber Hygiene" at the website: https://resources.sei.cmu.edu/library/asset-view.cfm?assetid= 540924. After viewing the video, list and describe five practices of good cyber hygiene discussed.

### Software Security and Ethics

Tom said, puzzled, "I understand why documentation is important. But why in the world is something like ethics placed in the software security area?" The Doc said, "Ethics is a theme that runs through many of the areas of cybersecurity, because a cybersecurity professional can sometimes lose their way without a clear statement about the rules for how to behave correctly. The problem is that ethics is subjective. For instance, white-hat hackers will break software products to identify zero-day vulnerabilities. They aim to identify any exposures that they can alert companies about. Those hackers genuinely believe that they are contributing to the common good of the profession. But, as well-intentioned as it might be, the people on the receiving end of these hacks might view that behavior as criminal, or at least unethical."

The Doc added, "There are no simple answers to the question of right or wrong. But the duty is clear. We have to give our students a baseline set of fundamental ethical principles to help them make the right decision." Lucy said, "So what you're talking about is the need to familiarize our students with the basic tenets of ethical conduct in cyberspace? That sounds pretty slippery to me, Doc. Are there any examples?"

The Doc said, "Thank you, Lucy. That's a good question. For example, your students must understand ethical issues like piracy and why protecting software from unauthorized use is important. It's also crucial that they have a good grounding on proper behavior regarding operating concerns like malware and safe program execution. The Software Security area is the only element within the common eight knowledge areas that includes a specific unit dedicated to ethics. But software is the one place where unethical behavior can be explicitly linked to harm. For instance, there's a concrete relationship between the price an organization would pay if it were found they were running software that had been pirated."

Tom said, "I know about that. There have been businesses that have lost everything because they were running pirated applications, even though the company owners didn't know that was going on. It was a few unethical employees who were the problem, but everybody paid." The Doc said sympathetically, "Yes, ethics is one of the few areas where the harm is real and obvious. So, as is the case with most of the other topics in the software security area, the focus in Ethics is on instilling proper behavior in the development and use of the software. There are five basic elements in the ethics knowledge area: (1) **ethical issues**, (2) **social aspects**, (3) **legal aspects**, (4) **vulnerability disclosure**, and (5) **what, when and why to test**."

Tom said, "They all seem to be pretty big-picture, except for the last two." Lucy, who had a legal background, said, "That makes sense since ethics is a big-picture issue. But you can always lay out basic principles for ethical behavior. Otherwise, the whole thing is in the eye of the beholder. Nonetheless, fundamental and commonly accepted tenets apply directly to computing, like the right to privacy and personal property protection. Those are universal, and they can be taught as simple rules of behavior, even to seventh graders. The same is true with social aspects. We all know there are guidelines for behaving properly in cyberspace, like no bullying or stalking, and there should be polite conduct in social media. We can list those and explain them as well. But, of course, we do that in almost any form of social studies class already."

Tom said, "I agree with Lucy. But what do we do about the legal issues? Should seventh graders learn about the law?" Lucy laughed and said, "I don't think that's what this is about. We teach students at all levels to be law-abiding. This is just a smaller and more special-ized set of rules. For instance, students need to know that trespassing in other people's space, as they do with simple hacking and even in physical instances like stealing other people's devices, is illegal. They also need to know the legal consequences of stalking and bullying. We don't have to teach them the legal procedure to make them aware of the consequences. We just need to discuss the more common viola-tions and what they represent in terms of punishments. In the second or third grade, we start doing that with offenses like stealing. So, this should be easy."

The Doc added, "That's true, Lucy, and very well stated. The last two items, testing and disclosure are more professional concerns and probably not appropriate to the levels we address. Both of them have to do with the constant bug hunting in the industry because of the problems associated with software defects. In one case, the issue relates to the responsibility for assurance testing at the appropriate point in the process. As you know, testing requires money. So, the aim is to get the proper balance between the need for assurance and the desire to keep the costs down. It's an ethical issue with too little assur-ance because the developer wants to increase their profits. The vulner-ability case is even more arcane. Once a vulnerability is discovered, it can be exploited. So the question is, when and to whom should you publicize the discovery? In some respects, everybody needs to know right away. But that also alerts the bad guys to the existence of an exploitable flaw before anybody can feasibly come up with the solution that will lock the door. There is no right answer except to say, 'be ethical when you disclose what you've found.'" But the answer to that problem has been kicked around for a long time without any hard-and-fast rule.

## EXERCISE

### SOFTWARE ETHICS CROSSWORD EXCHANGE

Do an internet search on the topic of software development ethical behaviors. As you explore related websites, make a list of 20 cases you feel are essential to software ethics. After compiling the list, visit the website: https://crosswordlabs.com/ and create a crossword puzzle with those words and statements about each. Then exchange your puzzle with a classmate. What did you learn about ethical behaviors from starting and completing crosswords?

The sun was setting on another day as the three of them cleaned up the room and put the chairs back in their proper place. Lucy was pleased. She said, "Thanks for helping Doc. I think we made a lot of progress today. So, there will be a big box of custard donuts waiting for you tomorrow."

# 4

## COMPONENT SECURITY

### It All Starts with Components

The gang got together a little late the next day because Lucy had to drop her kids off at summer camp. But she hadn't forgotten the donuts. The Doc was delighted. He said, "Did you get jelly?" Lucy said, "I have three jelly donuts for you. But first, you will have to explain why we are even looking at component security. I know it's an area in the CSEC. But the study of electronic components is way over the heads of K-12 students. So you'll get your first jelly donut only after you've satisfactorily explained to me what component security is."

The Doc looked wounded. He whined, "I can explain it better once I get my first sugar fix." Lucy said indulgently, "Oh well – I suppose so," and handed him a glistening little fat ball. The Doc took his first big bite and chewed thoughtfully. Then, finally, he said, "All digital things are collections of components. Those components enable every conceivable computerized purpose, and those purposes underwrite our world as a whole. The problem cybersecurity faces is that the architecture of digital things is becoming increasingly complex and, as a result, much more vulnerable. That's a crucial concern because our society is almost totally dependent on the reliable functioning of the components in our digital infrastructure."

The Doc added, "So if we want to trust the things that enable our way of life, we have to understand the basic design concepts and security considerations that motivate how we secure components." Tom said, puzzled, "I agree with Lucy. Focusing on the bits and pieces of the infrastructure pushes our teaching down to the hardware level. Isn't that a bridge too far?" The Doc said, "That's true, Tom. On the surface, component security DOES seem electronic. But at the secondary level, that knowledge area entails understanding the problems

DOI: 10.1201/9781003187172-4

associated with component design and testing, which is something you should have the students learn if you want to present the whole gamut of security considerations."

Tom said, "Design? How is component security related to design? It should be obvious. In a complex architecture, good design is the critical factor that ensures the integrity of the entire set of components. Hence, rational execution of the overall design process is vital."

Lucy said, "Let me get this straight. You're saying that component security is fundamentally a design problem, not an electronic one?" The Doc said, "Think about it. The choices you make when you assemble any given collection of components will determine the success or failure of the final product. So that's a design problem – right? Because, if those choices are improper or incorrectly made, you must assume that there will be security flaws in that architecture."

Lucy said, "I can see that. So, you're saying that the decisions you make about the components you select and how you combine them into a product are the determinant of how secure any product will be." The Doc said, "That's right." Tom said skeptically, "How do we teach something as abstract as THAT?" The Doc laughed and said, "There is one essential ability that's the root of good design, and that's functional decomposition."

Lucy sighed and said, "You're getting way past your headlights again, Doc. What the heck is functional decomposition, and why is it important?" The Doc laughed and said, "Functional decomposition is the process of peeling back the onion. The idea is to describe the architectural components from the top-down in increasingly more precise terms. So you break the elements of something into increasingly smaller constituent parts. That goes down to a level where every requisite behavior or functional property and the necessary interrelationships are fully characterized. In our terminology, that final collection of well-defined, inter-related, individual discrete behaviors, or modules is termed an 'architecture.'"

Tom said, "So we are just talking about a big-picture application of the same kind of principles that we were talking about in the software security area." The Doc said, "In essence, that's correct. Except for reverse engineering, a form of hacking, the other three knowledge units in component security are processes we talked about with software. But in the case of component security, the focus is specifically on the design, development, and assurance of tangible component architectures, not software."

Lucy said, "I think I see the difference. The topics that fall under component security focus more on the security of the physical and functional components of the system – right Doc?" The Doc said, "Perfect summary Lucy! Component security involves large-scale activities related to assuring any type of architecture. That includes such actions as lifecycle design, procurement, and assurance processes. The unique engineering activities are associated with discovering how a product is made and then using that information to re-produce the product. This topic is commonly called 'reverse engineering,' and that is something better studied at higher levels in the educational process."

Tom was looking at the CSEC table for component security. He said "the topics in this area are (1) **Component Design** – that we were just walking about, which seems to be the big-picture conceptual design process. It relates to creating secure component architectures, (2) **Component Procurement** – which looks like the things you'd need to know to ensure the safe purchase of digital items." Then, he stopped and added, "This is probably better taught at higher levels – right, Doc? But students need to be made aware of the special security considerations involved with purchased products not built. Then there is (3) **Component Testing**, which is the set of principles that underlie the quality and security assurance of component and product architectures. These aren't materially different from the assurance principles we looked at in the software security area. But what is (4) **Component Reverse Engineering**?"

The Doc said, "You got that exactly right, Tom. Reverse engineering is simply deducing an existing product's inherent structure and operation for either reproducing it or exploiting it. The actual practices for reverse engineering are way beyond what you would want to cover in junior and senior high school. But you should at least discuss what reverse engineering is and its implications for component security."

## Designing Secure Components

Lucy said, "So design is the first topic in this area. How is that different from what we just covered in software?" The Doc said, "On the surface, it isn't much. As we've seen, design at this level is an organizational process, not a technical one. In essence, the top-level view of the product documents all the things that it is meant to do. Therefore, the general intent of the design is that it has to be understandable to everybody involved in the process, not just the technical staff."

Tom said, "Could you be a little more specific. I can see that this is a process of dividing something into its constituent parts at one level for the purpose of further subdividing those parts at the next level. But how do you teach that?" The Doc said, "It's easy. You present it in its logical stages. The first stage breaks the product into its 'functional' components. In common terms, this is normally called a '**design**' view. Then the next step documents all of the operations that each component will have to perform and their interrelationship. That's called the **module** view. Next, the discrete behaviors associated with achieving the particular security objectives of the product are derived by addressing each module in assurance terms. Then, of course, there is also the necessary **physical** level view. The physical view documents the concrete arrangement of the constituent elements of the product. This is often known as a **schematic** view, which guides the construction process."

Tom said, "So how do you teach that?" The Doc said, "Good point Tom. To create a top-level rendering, the designers use the graphic approaches to describe the software functionality, primarily hierarchy diagrams. The aim is to create an inverted tree-like picture of the complete set of modules, or in CSEC terms, 'components,' that starts from the product's trunk down to the many sub-components at the leafiest end of the branch. So, the design process itself is iterative in that the depiction of the architecture is successively refined down to a point where there can be no possible misunderstanding of either the form of the components or what their interrelationships are in the tree."

"The description of these components is expressed in a way that relates directly to their real-world use. But that simple tree drawing exercise is no different from creating a complex architectural rendering of a component system."

"Tom said enthusiastically, "I get that! The easiest way to illustrate that to students, even one as far down as seventh grade, would be to start with an automobile or other common item like a ship or an airplane. Then, they could break it down into components like engine,

**Figure 4.1** Tom thinks of an inverted tree, to imagine what a complex software hierarchy diagram looks like.

transmission, and suspension. Then, if you wanted to illustrate the process, you could further break it down to the next level, like the engine, into its components like starter, distributor, and radiator. You can drill as far down as the students are capable of going. In my classes, juniors and seniors should even consider making modifications to the product, like adding or modifying components to soup up a car." The Doc said, "Absolutely correct, Tom! That is no different than the thinking that goes into any complex design project. They're just a lot more sophisticated in the real world now."

Good old practical Lucy said, "So the aim of the component design is to draw a detailed picture of the elements of the product. How is that different from the schematics drawn up for any other product in the physical universe?" The Doc said, "It isn't! The aim is to create a detailed picture of the item to be built. Once a detailed understanding is achieved, the designer creates a consistent top-level diagram that itemizes the product's features. That schematic depicts all basic components and relationships in detail as a coherent set of 'things.' The rendering then serves as a comprehensive roadmap for how the product will be built for a given application. Approaching the design in that way ensures against misunderstanding during the construction phase."

**Figure 4.2**    Tom thinks designing without having a detailed plan would be like putting a puzzle together without a picture.

He added, "That big-picture view helps identify any potential threats in the operational environment, and a comprehensive schematic also lets the designer think about relevant implementation and sustainment issues."

## EXERCISE

### MONEY FROM THE WALL

You have been asked to ensure the component security of a new ATM machine at the National Bank of Hooterville. First, draw a design diagram to represent the components of the machine. Start by drawing a top-level design, and then break down the functional elements as far as possible. *Hint: Think about the three functions of a computer; to accept inputs, do some sort of processing, and produce outputs.*

### Assuring the Architecture: Component Testing

The Doc continued with, "The final product of the design phase is a complete description of all of the build's pertinent traceability, testability, and feasibility requirements." Tom said, "That makes sense.

Just like with software security, component security should include a topic devoted solely to the practices required for assurance – right Doc?" The Doc said, "That's right, Tom, your students have to be familiar with the tools and methods used to ensure the security of given component architecture. That's just common sense."

Lucy said, "I can see why it would be important to know how tested and assured a product's components. That's the basis for trusting the product. But how is that news passed along to the customer?" The Doc said, "Ultimately, all of the components in every architecture must be tested and evaluated to confirm that they have been properly implemented and provide the expected functionality. But, more importantly, it must be demonstrated that whatever potential threats have been mitigated. That's the whole point of product assurance."

Lucy said, "Testing components sounds pretty complicated, Doc." The Doc said, "Just like software, there are always three stages involved in testing a complex artifact: unit, integration, and system." Lucy said, "Remind me again, what's a unit test?" The Doc said kindly, "Unit tests focus on the smaller, less complex aspects." Tom added, "Yes, the point of unit testing is to assure each component of the larger architecture, the smaller bit being called a 'module,' at the point where it's built." The Doc said, "That's right, you do that assurance by customizing each test to fit that particular module and that module only." Lucy said, "So, what does THAT involve?" The Doc took a bite out of his third jelly donut and said, "The testing process is just the scientific method. Essentially, the components are tested using a stated set of assumptions about what has to happen for the unit to be judged correctly. We call those assumptions a 'test case.' They are like the hypotheses in a scientific study." The Doc stopped chewing and added, "In the end, the point of unit testing is to determine whether a module performs as intended and satisfies all stated qualification criteria. That kind of testing is done down at the module level. You need to identify points of failure early because they are easier to correct then."

Tom said, "So, we can illustrate that process by having students list their assumptions about what should happen when they flip a light switch. The assumption is that the light will turn on when the switch on the wall is flipped. But the light itself might be turned off, or it might be on one of those fancy wall timers where it doesn't come on except at certain times. The student could verify the switch's performance under all three of those assumptions, and if the light comes on when the switch is flipped, it passes the test. If it doesn't, then the other two conditions have to be investigated and verified." The Doc said, delighted, "That is a perfect example of a component test case, and it illustrates how you use test cases to get a better idea about the contingencies that might affect the component. In that respect, it is just like the testing processes used in the software." Lucy said wryly, "Like you said, testing's just a practical application of the scientific method."

Tom was reading the CSEC. He said, "It makes the point that module testing is different than security testing." The Doc said, "Right again, Tom. Security testing asks the question 'Is this component trustworthy?' Thus conventional security testing methods such as stress and fuzz tests are utilized for security testing. The aim is to find out what happens beyond the established tolerances." Lucy said, "What the heck does that mean? Are you intentionally trying to break it?" The Doc said, "Absolutely! The aim is to identify what we call 'exceptions.' Those are any severe problems that might occur just over the boundary between regular operation and exceptional demands. Examples of a condition like that would be where catastrophic component failure occurs at the edge of normal operating limits."

Tom said, puzzled, "Why is THAT important?" The Doc said, "Security tests of this type are a vital part of the entire cybersecurity process. They identify those security problems hidden just beyond the periphery of normal component performance. You always want a little margin of error if there is a disastrous failure. So, if you know where that point occurs, you can adjust the operating parameters to ensure a safe operating range."

Lucy said, "That might be a fun exercise. We could use one of those foot-operated air pumps to blow up a rubber ducky to the manufacturer's prescribed pressure. Then we could have the students record the number of pumps it took afterward to pop Mr. Ducky. That would tell us exactly what the margin of error would be when blowing up a pool float." The Doc said, "Brilliant Lucy!! That is the exact way stress testing is done, except the tested components aren't wearing little sailor hats."

Lucy said, "So you're saying that component testing methods are no different from conventional software testing methods?" The Doc said, "In general, that's correct; however, penetration tests are also. Those are a novel way of looking at security questions." Lucy said, "You've talked about those before. How do they apply to components?" The Doc said, "Penetration tests aim to find and exploit vulnerabilities in a component, or an architecture. A good penetration test will help the organization understand how attackers could compromise an entire architecture by attacking a particular component."

Tom said enthusiastically, "I did a few of those in college. Penetration tests are usually scenario-driven. You try to think of anything that could go wrong, and when you attempt to exploit it. Penetration tests are frequently done through automation. But the key to success is creativity. The idea is to think about how the component works and imagine every conceivable weakness you might exploit. For example, we could have the students write down how they might break into the locked classroom. You might even have them try their ideas out. Of course, that would be with strict warnings that this is an exercise, and you are not encouraging them to do that in real life. If you decide to try controlled break-ins, though, it would also be a lovely way of illustrating the principles of ethical hacking."

## EXERCISE

### CATCHING VULNERABILITIES BEFORE THEY CATCH YOU

Assemble into groups of no more than three. Each group should design its own data company (for example, a social media platform or a telemarketing company). First, describe the company's component architecture. Second, each group should design test cases for three architecture components. Finally, develop a penetration test on another group's company. You will need to think about the security infrastructure and where the potential vulnerabilities are likely to be and think of strategies to exploit these vulnerabilities.

## Buying Components Instead of Making Them

Lucy said, "Okay, Doc, procurement is the next topic. I don't see how security and purchasing go together. So, we can skip this, right?" The Doc said, "You're partially right, Lucy. The assurance of a chain of trust in products acquired via a complex and remote set of suppliers is built around the assurance of correctness. That process is beyond anything that would normally be studied anywhere but a business school. But it would be helpful if students understood that the digital toys they purchase might have hazards intentionally built into them. So, they should be aware of the general issues of product acquisition and the potential pitfalls they might represent. So, it would be helpful if they were at least aware of how supply chains work, what could go wrong in the process and how to mitigate any potential pitfalls by exercising simple common sense."

Tom said, "Okay – I accept that. But what's the problem? Why should I be concerned about security when I buy my next cell phone?" The Doc said, "It's like that old saying about the weakest link. Because the development and manufacturing of that cell phone took place within a complex supply chain, the reliability and integrity of the product are critical concerns. If that supply chain is ever compromised, then malicious actors can embed nasty things in the product, and you would never know it. They could listen to your conversations, steal your private information, or even sabotage the phone's operation from some dark corner of the internet. The people who make the phone wouldn't know they were selling you a malicious device because they never intended to put the malware in the component. They just didn't check closely enough to determine whether one of their subcontractors had."

Lucy squealed, "That's outrageous!! How could any reputable manufacturer let something like that happen!!??" The Doc said, "Unfortunately, most of your modern digital products are produced via a chain of suppliers who contribute some bit or another to the total package that you are buying. The problem is that the person who puts their nameplate on the product often doesn't know what small suppliers exist at the bottom of their supply chain. They only know the top-level suppliers with who they deal directly. The seller isn't sure what components they are integrating into products, let alone who made them with complex products. Thus, the CSEC's component procurement knowledge unit activities are geared toward giving people some general awareness of why it's important to ensure strict oversight and control over disparate objects as they move through the supply chain. This is an important consideration because a malicious item introduced by a less visible company at a low level in the supply chain can become a make-it-or-break-it security flaw in the final product. That's what I'm talking about here."

Tom said, "So what can we do about it at the junior and senior high school level? There is no way the kids would understand or even care about the strategic management of supply chains." The Doc laughed and said, "Of course, supply chains are vast, and commercial product assurance is a strategic policy issue, not something relevant for a high school student. But students need to understand those potentially malicious items are embedded in the many odd digital gadgets they love to buy. So, the reputation of the supplier is a critical concern. Therefore, it's essential to know how every potential supplier approaches security. The lesson would aim to ensure that your students are fully aware of supply chain risks vis-à-vis the things they purchase."

Lucy piped up with, "I like that! I could see dividing the class into small groups and having each group work on a separate part of a larger school project, like building a homecoming float, decorations for a dance, or anything with many parts involved. We could tell them they get extra credit if they slip something that wasn't supposed to be there into the final product, like a hidden Easter egg. Then we could have them all work on putting together the final product and get extra credit if they found somebody else's Easter egg. That would illustrate the problem if not provide much of a solution. It would be an excellent introduction to supply chains, though, don't you think, Doc?"

## EXERCISE

### FINDING A NEEDLE IN A HAYSTACK

Make a list of five hardware components in your computer (e.g., hard drive). Then, do an internet search of the countries that make those components and write them down next to each component. Next, search for possible cybersecurity concerns related to computer components manufactured in those countries. Finally, write a summary of what you discovered.

The Mystery of Reverse Engineering

The Doc said, "That's a superb idea, Lucy, and it would illustrate the problem exactly as we intend. As Tom said, untrustworthy supply chains are a global problem that are only made worse by the increasing complexity of the digital products we purchase. So, we need to plant the seed of skepticism as early as possible about secure construction processes, even if it's building a homecoming float. What you're suggesting would illustrate the problem. Then, we can leave the solutions for later on in the education process."

Tom said, "So what about reverse engineering? That's last. I know what both words mean, but I have no idea what reverse engineering is." The Doc said, "Neither does anybody else, except perhaps the real technology fans. Reverse engineering is the same process that a mechanic might follow to understand a new engine. In the mechanic's case, reverse engineering would involve disassembling a new and unknown engine to understand exactly how it works."

Lucy said, "So what's the point of that? I don't see how it applies to security." The Doc said, "Reverse engineering lets you see the inner workings of components that would otherwise be a black box. The key condition is that the reverse-engineer has little or no knowledge of the components or the product's architecture under study when they begin the process. So, the product is deconstructed to see how each of the components works and their architectural interrelationships."

Tom said, "I still don't see why that is relevant to component security?" The Doc laughed and said, "At our level reverse engineering is just a term that your students need to know about, not something they need to learn to do. Reverse engineering's basic goal is 'understanding' versus 'making changes' like most security exploits. That distinction has to be kept in mind when thinking about components. With components, reverse engineering is done to learn about the components and architecture of a given product. In its practical form, reverse engineering tries to understand how the product operates to attack it. So, a lot of effort makes it harder for the reverse engineer to do that in the professional world."

Lucy, who was becoming quite good at teaching this, said, "I can see an exercise that might be interesting to illustrate that process. We could divide the class into two teams. The aim would be to do what

I assign, like a Raspberry Pi program, so the other team can't figure out how they did it. Then they would exchange their final product. The prize would go to the team that tells me how the other team did it." Tom said, "I LIKE that!! I could even do it by requiring the same project but in C++. That would be a perfect way to learn the basics of the reverse engineering process." The Doc said, "Bravo, both of you. That is not a lot different in concept than what is going on in cyberspace right now."

The Three Musketeers felt very satisfied by their day's work. They had managed to put together a curriculum piece for a knowledge area rarely covered in higher education. They felt like they had gotten the essential educational point across. Lucy noticed how carefully Tom and The Doc were cleaning up after themselves. She said, "I'll bring two boxes of donuts for tomorrow because the Connection Security knowledge area will make for a very long day."

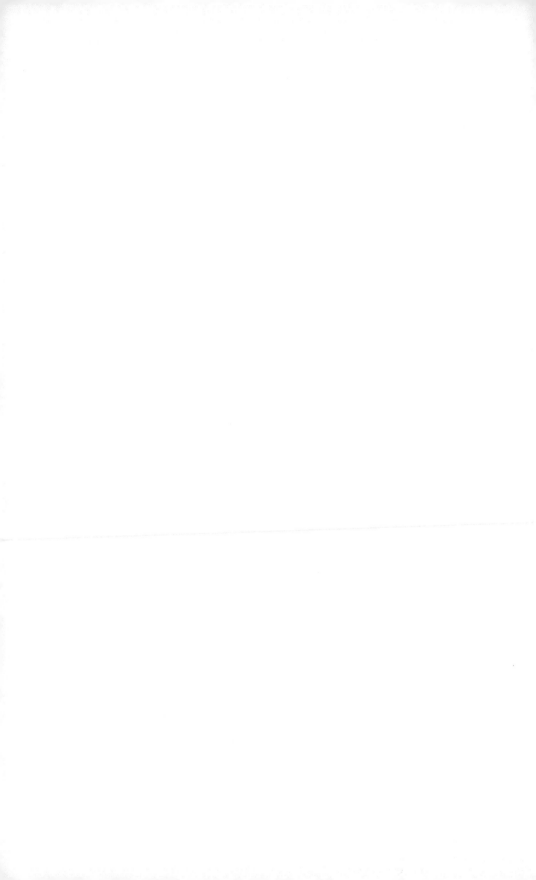

# 5

## CONNECTION SECURITY

The following day was cold and rainy. So Tom brought a big container of hot coffee, and Lucy showed up with TWO boxes of donuts. The Doc was overjoyed. All three could see that Connection Security was one of the longest sections in the CSEC. So, they got right down to business. Lucy said, "Okay Doc, I know what network security is. We don't teach that at the junior high level, but Tom covers some of that in high school. It involves things like CISCO academies, right?"

Tom said, "That's right. So, why is this even an issue here? We've been teaching people about data communications since well before the internet came along?" The Doc was savoring his first jelly donut as he said, "Good point Tom, but the Connection Security knowledge area of the CSEC is a lot broader in scope than simple network security. It encompasses *all* of the processes, practices, and technologies that we utilize to defend networks or any set of interconnected computers. It also includes the data communications software and all of the basic concepts of remote transmission, like the internet of things which comprises a lot more than just the conventional vision of networks."

Lucy said, "I don't see the difference." The Doc said, "Traditional network security protects electronic interaction between two endpoints. That is indeed a data communication process, but it doesn't come close to encompassing all of the current issues associated with the electronic transmission of data."

Lucy still looked puzzled. So, the Doc explained, "The attack surface of a data communications system amounts to the sum of every way that an outside party could compromise it. That includes the normal concerns of unauthorized access and anything related to subversion of functioning. Since those potential threats are as diverse as the human mind can conceive and they can appear at any time, or originate from any place in the world, connection security might be the most difficult challenge of the cybersecurity process."

DOI: 10.1201/9781003187172-5

**Figure 5.1** Tom's classroom was ready to continue the cybersecurity discussion with plenty of coffee and donuts on hand.

Both Lucy and Tom continued to look confused. So, the Doc finished with, "The specific mission of connection security is to protect remote communications from unauthorized modification, destruction, or disclosure. As such, connection security has the unenviable task of guaranteeing that an exponentially growing number of anonymous exploits will not impact a diverse and widely dispersed information infrastructure. The range, diversity, scope, and timing of those incidents and the medium's complexity make network security a compelling and difficult challenge." Again, both Tom and Lucy looked aghast. Finally, Tom muttered under his breath, "I hadn't thought of it that way."

The Doc was on a roll. He said, "Modern connectivity allows anything from phishing to cyber-terrorism to be delivered to your doorstep on every device in your house... from personal voice assistants to surreptitious updates of your internet-enabled TV set. Moreover, those new connection features comprise a much broader risk than the simple challenge of just securing transmission endpoints. Hence, connection security focuses on assuring the full range of communication technologies in our complex society."

Lucy said skeptically, "That's a pretty amorphous collection of things. How can any reasonable person expect to do that successfully."

But, the Doc said, "You can get the ball rolling if you categorize the problem by the type of threat. Connection security falls into four categories. First and foremost, it has to protect your confidential information. But it also has to safeguard the physical transmission medium from harm and ensure that the particular network's components are operating properly and achieving their intended purpose. Finally, connection security must ensure that the information transmitted retains its fundamental integrity and purpose throughout the transmission process. That latter responsibility involves assuring the robustness and integrity of the media that records and retains the information."

Tom said, "Okay, I understand that. You're saying that there are four fundamental parts to the connection security mission. First, there's classic access control which was the mission even back in the 1970s and 1980s when confidentiality was primarily a mainframe concern. But the latter three issues apply to everything in the current internet of things. So how would anybody address something like the reliability or robustness of an internet-enabled doorbell camera?"

The Doc said in a serious tone, "Good point! When people think of connection security, they usually just think about traditional devices. Whereas connection security encompasses a diverse range of internet-enabled technologies, many of whom are interconnected and constitute a potential source of compromise. As a result, the problem of connection security has to be viewed through a much wider lens. And many of the critical activities don't directly involve technical work."

Lucy said, "Explain that, please." The Doc took another bite of his donut, chewed appreciatively, and said, "For instance, good policy and effective procedures are needed to coordinate any connection security process. Even such indirect actions as routine training and awareness are necessary to ensure the ongoing capability of the network staff and users. Consequently, the connection security function cannot be approached as a strictly technical exercise. Instead, connection security entails an all-inclusive mix of mutually supporting topics. All of these need to be familiar to your students."

Lucy said, "So, what are those, exactly? What do we need to present? I don't think computer science theory is appropriate in a junior high classroom. So, what do we concentrate on?"

The Doc said, "Connection security is enabled by consciously designed and implemented controls." Tom said, "Do you mean controls as discussed in the other sections? You know – specific discrete behaviors that you design and implement to ensure that something always happens in a certain way."

The Doc said, "That's exactly it, Tom!! Security breaches occur when the security situation isn't comprehensively or adequately controlled. That includes the failure to ensure the correctness of all network interactions. Consequently, there is an obligation to ensure that a tangible control has addressed every likely threat. In essence, the network operation seeks to guarantee that all critical communication interactions, both internal and external, in the overall process are correct and proper. The term 'robustness' is often used to describe that state."

Lucy said, "What do you mean by robustness? How do we ensure quality like that? I need some tangible examples if I have to teach something as vague as that." The Doc said approvingly, "Of course you do, Lucy. The most recognizable example of a general control is a firewall, which is placed on a network strictly to ensure safe data handling across the protection perimeter. It does that by utilizing specifically programmed instructions. Installing one of those on a system ensures robust access control."

Tom said, "Okay, that covers access control, but what about the concrete parts of the system?" The Doc said, "Perhaps the most recognizable example of a hardware control might be the router, the tangible gateway between your network and the rest of the world. Other basic examples of control categories that you might want to familiarize your students with include protection measures such as encryption, anti-virus, and anti-malware software and even something as humble as routine network maintenance."

Lucy said, "I guess I can see that. You tell us that we need to focus our teaching on the commonplace mechanisms for mitigating connection risks, right?" Tom jumped in at that point. He said, "That's nice in concept Doc. But the reality is that we cannot react as fast as advances in technology push us, so we're always forced to play catch-up. That makes it hard to focus on any given technology or product."

The Doc said approvingly, "You are right there, Tom. The environment is ever-changing. So, it requires a continuous identification, analysis, and response process. As a result, there has to be a formal mechanism to guide and ensure the necessary oversight." He stopped and added, "Fortunately, we have a standard set of well-defined best practices developed over time. These are aimed at making the connection process harder to subvert and easier to understand. That is what the CSEC gives us."

### The CSEC Connection Security Knowledge Areas

Good old practical Lucy said, "So, let's look at those topics." Tom studied the document and said, "It looks like there are eight general topics in the connection security knowledge area: **Physical Media** – which I assume encompasses the basic signaling and transmission equipment, **Physical Interfaces and Connectors** – which probably focuses on the actual interconnection bits and pieces, and then there's **Hardware Architecture** – which I guess involves the currently accepted categories of generic hardware structures, **Distributed Systems Architecture** – which has to be the basic concepts that underlie distributed systems, and then there is **Network Architecture** – which must be the fundamental set of network connectivity concepts, **Network Implementations** – which has to do with basic network architecture implementation concerns, **Network Services** – which are the different models for implementing practical connectivity, and finally there is **Network Defense** – which encompasses all of the methods and models for effectively protecting networks."

The Doc said approvingly, "Couldn't have summarized it better." Lucy said, "Well then… let's get started trying to fit this laundry list of topics into our junior high and senior high classrooms. I guess we should take them in the order that the CSEC presents them."

### Topic One: The Physical Components of the Network

Tom said, "Okay, Doc, exactly what are they talking about when they use the term 'Physical network?'" The Doc laughed and said, "It's the tangible part of the signal transmission process. Simply put, it's any physical bit of communication media that enables the transportation of messages from one computing device to another. Those are things like the cables that interconnect the numerous devices to let them interact with each other. You don't transmit data without using a physical device, even if it's Wi-Fi. So, consequently, the physical communication equipment is the foundation on which the entire process rests."

Lucy said, "That's still a little too global for my tastes. Specifically, what are we talking about here? What do we need to discuss." The Doc said, "Networks transmit data from point to point in a prearranged fashion. The physical network equipment serves as the infrastructure to allow the network's many physical endpoints to connect and communicate."

Tom said, "Like what – for example?" The Doc said, "Various physical media are employed in the transmission process. They vary in essential considerations such as cost, bandwidth capacity, transmission time, and ease of installation. Examples of physical media include offline storage media such as recordable DVDs, USB flash drives, or even the cables that interconnect things. There are four sub-areas in the Physical Media knowledge area: (1) *Transmission in a medium* – which describes how the physical equipment used for signaling works, (2) *Shared and point-to-point media* – which describes the characteristics of the different physical transmission devices, (3) *Sharing models* – the traditional set-ups for sharing between multiple clients, and (4) *Common technologies* – this last one simply lists the various examples of the physical communication media discussed in this section."

Tom said, "So if we teach this, we need to have concrete examples to show and tell, right?" Lucy said, "Yes, the students have to be able to see and touch the actual components." Tom said, "That would be easy. We could keep examples of routers, hubs, switches, and associated cabling in our classroom. I could conduct a session where we do a grand tour of each technology, pointing out the specific parts of the item that perform the desired function. The idea would be to familiarize the student with the actual mechanism's physical form and how it fulfills its basic purpose."

Lucy added enthusiastically, "Then we could relate the individual characteristics of each of the technologies to the commonly accepted ways they should be physically arranged, like a star or ring, and even have the students critique the effectiveness of each layout."

Tom said, "Yes, we could have them decide what technologies work best in a star versus a ring network." Lucy said, "That's called topology – right? Of course, that might be over the heads of the average junior high student. But I suppose some of yours could push it that far. Our students need to come away from this section appreciating how networks are composed of physical objects. Networks have real-world characteristics that can be strengths and weaknesses depending on how they are arrayed."

## EXERCISE

## IDENTIFYING TRANSMISSION MEDIA

Go to your school's computer lab and identify the type of transmission media and devices that make up that network. What kind of transmission media was used? Did you see any switches, hubs, or routers? If so, what was the distance between each device connected by the media? Try to answer the question as to why one type of media was used over another.

### Topic Two: Physical Interfaces and Connectors

The Doc, who had been watching the interchange with approval, said, "That is correct, and congratulations to you. You are both getting the hang of this. Next, we have to look at how we can teach students about the existing pipelines that the data travels down. That means we have to help them understand the essential characteristics of the media that interconnects a network's physical objects, including the material that those connectors are physically composed of and the common standards that define those characteristics. There are three simple sub-areas in the Physical Interfaces and Connectors topic area:

1. *Hardware characteristics and materials* – which look at the aspects of the connection media, as well as the strengths and weaknesses of the various cables that are used in data transmission,
2. *Standards* are the authoritative industry models for data transmission media and connectors.
3. *Common interconnectors* – which simply focus on the various types of standard connections that are currently in use."

Tom said, "Let me get this straight. Why do students need to learn something as trivial as the hardware characteristics and materials of a cable? What value is there in something like that?" The Doc said, "Well, realistically, most people don't need to think about this unless they are setting up a network. But the fact is that the type of connection medium determines the network's performance characteristics. So, everybody needs to understand that there are speed and distance limitations in any physical arrangement of components based on the transmission characteristics of the medium."

Lucy said, "Okay, Doc, give me an example, and I'll give YOU another donut." The Doc chuckled as he was reaching for his next jelly-filled delight and said, "For instance, there are three choices when it comes to cabling, twisted pair, coaxial, and fiber optic cables, and the performance of your network will be vastly different based on which medium you choose. So, your students need at least to understand the tradeoffs between the three of them. For instance, this is the point in the educational process where you would teach them about Ethernet, which is a fairly simple explanation at the top and has an infinite number of tangible examples you can use. Then, as a contrast, you can compare Ethernet performance to fiber optic cabling and illustrate how the latter supports high-speed data communications. The comparison ought to be enlightening for your students, and it is something that even junior high kids should be able to understand because most of them spend their spare time streaming videos and playing games."

Lucy said, "Okay, I see that. But what the heck do standards have to do with any of this. I don't see wasting my time on something better discussed in an engineering school, not a junior high." The Doc laughed and said, "Standards are nothing more than specifications of how something has to be built to be used by everybody. They are just the specifications of what everybody agrees has to be done to communicate in a certain medium. For example, you would have a Tower of Babel situation if there weren't commonly agreed on ways to interconnect physical devices. The pin arrangements in an RJ45 connector are nothing appropriate even at the secondary level unless you are teaching it in some voc-tech program. But the students DO need to know who makes standards for electrical equipment, why that's important, and what some of the most important specifications are."

Lucy said, "So, what's the practical reason for a standard?" The Doc chuckled and said, "The physical world has to have compatibility for electronic devices to talk to each other." Then he stopped and added, "That wasn't always the case for data transmission. Until the advent of client-server technology, every manufacturer had unique physical ways of interconnecting. So mainframes could only communicate with other mainframes from the same manufacturer. Common connection standards changed that. Now you can interconnect devices such as hosts, switches, and routers from many suppliers as long as they adhere to the same specifications for physical connection."

Tom said, "So what you're saying is that our students need to understand that everybody has to be on the same page regarding physical layout and everyday functioning, or there wouldn't be any data communication. The standards simply serve as the mechanism by which the industry communicates that common agreement." The Doc said, "Exactly, Tom, you can illustrate that by presenting a simple section that describes the key standards issued by the Telecommunications Industry Association. The TIA is the authorized standards maker for these types of devices."

Lucy said, "I guess I understand that, and I'll bet the last topic, common interconnectors, simply does the same thing for the end-connectors that allow those cable types to be plugged into the various pieces of equipment. In the network." The Doc said, "Excellent, Lucy. Connectors allow the transmission media to be physically connected with the different pieces of equipment used in a typical network. That involves a variety of connections. The most common one is the RJ45 connector that everybody has seen hundreds of times because it looks and works like the connectors you use for your telephones. And, of course, they look that way because the telephone company originally developed RJ45. That might be the only thing you should concentrate on at the secondary level since the RJ45 connector is the physical plug for Ethernet."

Tom said, "Okay, Ethernet is so common I could see why that connector would be the one thing you would want to concentrate on. But what should we teach?" The Doc said, "That standard specifies the pin arrangements or, in simple terms, the positions of the actual plugs that connect the various wires in an Ethernet cable." Lucy said, "So all we would have to do is put up a single graphic that shows the prongs of an RJ-45 connector and their purpose." Then she stopped and added, "I know they aren't prongs like in an electrical cord. But they serve the same function. They plug into a slot to complete a circuit, except there are eight of them rather than the two in an electrical cord."

The Doc laughed and said, "Couldn't have said it better, Lucy, and that's a great idea. All you would have to do is discuss what each pin brings to the party. That's the proper term, by the way, not prong. There are eight of them in an RJ45 connector. Two are not used at all, and the other six have to do with transmitting data. So your students would get an idea about the general process of data communication if they simply memorized the specific purpose of each pin."

## EXERCISE

## STANDARDIZING THE WAY DATA IS TRANSMITTED

When considering the security of transition media, three considerations need to be made:

- The transmission is based on Ethernet.
- The transmission is based on Wi-Fi.
- Transmission is based on Wi-Fi with Bluetooth available.

Each of the considerations is supported by an industry standard. Identify the standard for each consideration and describe how it would be used to ensure data security as it is being transmitted.

### Topic Three: Physical Architecture: The Tangible Part of the Network

Tom said, "It looks like the next three topics relate to architecture." The Doc said, "That's right, Tom, since the design is how you build a network. Therefore, it's important to understand network architecture." Lucy asked the same question she had every time the misleading term "architecture" was brought up. Finally, she said, "Tell me specifically what you mean by architecture in this case, Doc."

The Doc said, "Good point in particular here, Lucy. Since the implications for architecture are different than they were in the component areas. In the case of networks, 'architecture' refers to the tangible realization of a design concept. In that respect, the way we use the term here is much closer to the concept of architecture when it comes to buildings."

Tom said, puzzled, "Okay, explain THAT then." The Doc said, "At the bare metal level, the physical embodiment of a network architecture lies in the logic circuit design on the chip. While in its broadest sense, the tangible realization of a network architecture involves global multicomponent systems. So, architecture as a generic term refers to the specification of the exact set of components and associated interfaces that will be implemented at whatever level of tangible realization the network will be viewed. Be it microscopic implementations on the chip or in transatlantic fiber optic cables. Physically, architecture implies that the physical parts-and-pieces of the network, like cables, switches, and hubs, and the intrinsic logic are known and how they are arranged and interact is fully and completely fulfilled."

Both Lucy and Tom looked like they were trying to relate what the Doc had just said to something tangible. So, he continued, "In many ways, what I just described is the process that you go through when you design any physical structure, like a building. Architects conceptualize the 'things' that need to be in the building to fulfill its purpose, as well as the shape and function of the rooms in the building that contains them. The objective of the architectural process is always to craft the most effective structure to achieve the intents of the users. Then, once the design is complete, the developers simply implement it. But the tangible form of the thing has to be fully understood before it can be built. That is the role of an architectural rendering, or what you might call a blueprint."

Tom said, "That sounds relatively straightforward and easy. The designer lays out the elements that best satisfy the purpose, and then the builder builds them." The Doc said, "That's how the process looks on the surface. But the primary challenge with hardware architectures is that electronic components have to obey the limitations imposed by the physical world. For example, it is easy to talk about communication between two endpoints in the abstract. However, it is much more of a challenge if the Pacific Ocean is in-between. That makes hardware architecture a pragmatic design activity at its base.

Consequently, there are three sub-areas in the Hardware Architecture topic area:

1. *Standard Architectures* – which refer to the commonly accepted architectural approaches and the advantages of each.
2. *Hardware interface standards* are the various real-world hardware interface standards that a designer must be aware of.
3. *Common architectures* present the most common examples of standardized hardware technologies. That includes such omnipresent technologies as Ethernet and other kinds of connector standards."

Lucy said, "Okay, I'll bite. What in the world is the advantage of a standard architecture?" Surprisingly, Tom answered her. He said, "We learned that in the B-School. Over the years, the efforts by the industry to standardize computerized equipment, particularly network components, have significantly improved the compatibility, and efficiency of global networks. More importantly, it has also lowered the cost of support and maintenance."

Lucy turned to Tom and said, "Okay, smarty-pants, what are some examples?" Tom thought and said, "Well, I'd say Bluetooth is the most recognizable standard for most of our students because they have that on their phones. The IEEE, one of the contributing bodies to the CSEC, standardized that technology in the 1980s as IEEE 802.15.1. It is maintained by a special body called the Bluetooth Special Interest Group. And of course, on the software side, there's HTTP which is RFC 7540 in its latest incarnation, and HTML, which is ISO/IEC 15445. The point is that we can engage the students if we talk about how the development of common standards makes it possible for them to post messages on Facebook."

The Doc said, "That's very good, Tom. The next topic in this category is Hardware Interface Standards, which we can handle differently. The purpose of interface standards is to ensure compatibility among devices, like computers, output devices, printers, and network equipment. But those standards concentrate strictly on the hardware interfaces, so the electrical engineering content is probably more appropriate at the university level. Still, you can show the students drawings of the standard hardware interfaces that interconnect two components, such as the plugs and sockets that attach Ethernet cables to devices, which we just discussed. Or, they could identify the purpose of the pins on DVA adaptors." Lucy said, "Terminology Doc, what's a DVA?" The Doc laughed and said, "Direct Voltage Adapter, you know, the old nine-pin connectors you used to hook up peripherals like printers. That's been mainly replaced by USBs and wireless, another lovely example of standardized hardware interfaces."

Tom said, "So we are talking about the same teaching approach. We would have sample Ethernet, DVA, or RGB connectors that the students could look at, and we could talk about why we need to standardize the plugs and sockets on the hardware they interconnect." Lucy said, "I can see that. We might start with Legos to illustrate why it's important to standardize the shape of the interface. You know, you can't force a square Lego on a round one." She chuckled at her joke.

The Doc chuckled along with Lucy and said, "Very Good!!! That is the point of the last topic in this area, Common Architectures." Lucy said, "What are you talking about, Doc?" The Doc said, "Just like a Lego set, the tangible architecture of a system refers to both the physical components and the things that interconnect them. There can be a lot of Legos in the box, but they can only be connected based on their physical characteristics. So Legos pieces have to have pre-defined

**Figure 5.2**  Tom pictures Doc's example about system architecture.

built-in compatibility before you can set about building a Lego castle. If there was no standardization for the pieces, for instance, the indentations of one piece didn't match the edges and plugs of the other, then there would be no castle. That's true with any physical interconnection. So you could illustrate incompatibility by simply asking the students to build something using two or three different sizes of Legos. The problems they would face would be a perfect illustration of why physical incompatibility has to be dealt with through the standardization of the tangible building blocks. You could easily drive that point home for them by having another group of students build the same castle using a set of Legos that all meet the same standard."

### Topic Four: Building a Distributed System

Lucy, who seemed to have appointed herself the unofficial secretary of the group, said, "The next item is distributed systems. Tell me exactly what those are, Doc, since I know both words, but I still don't understand what they're talking about here." The Doc laughed and said, "I can count on you to cut right to the chase Lucy. The term distributed system just denotes an array of diverse computing equipment interconnected via a centralized processor. The software that enables that interconnection is typically termed 'NetWare,' or a 'network operating system.'"

Tom added brightly, "The most recognizable example of the distributed concept is the internet. Consequently, knowledge of the general principles of a distributed network and its components and their interconnection methods is a must for anybody living in the modern world. Still, students need to understand that the internet isn't the only networking method and TCP/IP is not the only protocol."

The Doc added, "That's right, Tom. As the concept grew, the interconnected components of a network were distributed over an increasingly wider geographic area, from local area networks, called LANS, to wide area networks, termed WANS, and even to the creation of virtual private networks called VPNs." He took a big bite of his next donut and continued with, "At its simplest, distributed architecture describes the interconnection of multiple CPUs into some form of unified entity. The broadest implementation of that concept is the World Wide Web."

The Doc took another bite and said, "Sounds simple, doesn't it? But the challenge with that kind of interconnectedness lies in the wide variety of computer hardware, none of which is directly compatible with each other. So it isn't a matter of simply wiring everything together. Instead, we have to devise an approach that will allow all of the diverse hardware entities on a network to talk to each other. That interconnection of inherently incompatible devices is enabled by the concept of packet-based protocols, the most common of which is the transmission control protocol (TCP). But there is also the simpler User Datagram Protocol, and of course, there's the HyperText Transfer Protocol or HTTP. Each of these protocols has specific characteristics. So, the focus of the teaching should be on comparing each approach, and the implications in terms of the security of the data they transmit."

Lucy said, "So what's involved here, Doc?" The Doc said, "There are seven sub-topic areas in the CSEC's Distributed Systems Architecture:

1. *Network Architectures, General Concepts*: this looks at how to design and construct an enterprise network.
2. *World Wide Web*: protocols that enable the internet.
3. *The internet*: topics that discuss its history and evolution.
4. *Protocols and layering*: this looks at the operational layers of the International Standards Organization's Open Systems Interconnection Model.

Then there are a couple of areas we will not address at the secondary level:

5. *High-performance computing*: how to aggregate resources into supercomputers.
6. *Hypervisors and cloud computing implementations*: this looks at the various service concepts like Infrastructure as a Service (IaaS), Software as a Service (SaaS), or Platform as a Service (PaaS).
7. *Vulnerabilities*: this is an extremely important topic because it concentrates on the attack surface of a network."

Lucy said, "Well, the first topic is, 'Network Architectures General Concepts.' what the heck is that?" The Doc laughed and said, "It's no small undertaking to design and build an efficient and effective enterprise network. People have to make many options and decisions that people have to make, such as where to locate the network nodes, what kind of bandwidth is required, whether to run Ethernet to each node, right down to simple things like whether and how to implement wireless. There are also decisions about the brand of firewall, router, switch, and other types of network products??"

Tom added, "Not to mention the security considerations like the kind of intrusion detection system and the programmed responses. So, the best thing we can do is present this as the management and design project." The Doc added, "That's right, Tom. But the nuts-and-bolts of load balancing and bandwidth calculations are way out of the purview of secondary school students. Those topics might even be too complex for undergraduates. But it is important that secondary students are at least aware that performance issues must be considered when implementing a network."

Lucy said like a light bulb had gone off in her head, "We don't need to get into the nitty-gritty of networking technology to demonstrate that topic. It can be demonstrated by discussing the performance considerations involved in constructing a network. We can structure it as if the student were buying a car. You can have students list and justify what they want their new car to do in the light of practical considerations, like does the buyer have a lot of kids or live in a place with bad weather? You know what I mean. You could help students understand that there are tradeoffs between what you want in terms of performance and the constraints of the situation. Those all have to be resolved before deciding on the right vehicle. That's what enterprise network architects do, right?"

Tom said, "That would be a fun exercise, Lucy, because students are all interested in hot cars. But how does that tie in with the internet? Which are the next three topics." The Doc said, "Well, the internet is the ultimate distributed system. So to be fully knowledgeable about that topic, a properly educated student has to know something about its basic structure. In particular, they have to be able to tell the difference between the World Wide Web and the internet."

Lucy said, astonished, "I thought those two were the same thing." The Doc said, "It's a common misconception. But they are not the same. The *web* is all of humanity's information, recorded on many sites and pages created over time. The *internet* is the unitary transmission system that gives users access to that information. In essence, the World Wide Web is all the books in the library. At the same time, the internet is the library itself, including the card catalogs and shelving system that facilitate finding the right book. Protocols that enable that search like HTTP and the URLs that label individual books are the things that allow people to find what they're looking for among the infinite number of books in that library."

Tom said excitedly, "The easiest way to teach that would be through the next topic, the history, and evolution of the internet's structure." The Doc said, "Excellent point, Tom. In concept, the internet is the world's largest distributed system. But like all systems, it embodies a common set of characteristics. Those characteristics are what your students need to learn." Tom said, puzzled, "And just what are those characteristics?"

The Doc said, "The internet's standard protocols and layering concepts are the fundamental things a student needs to know. Those are the inventions that had to be discovered to create the internet. DARPA developed the TCP, internet protocol, called TCP/IP, in the late 1970s, and Tim Berniers-Lee at CERN connected that to the hypertext transfer protocol in the late 1980s to create what we think of as the web. At the same time, the International Standards Organization, which everybody calls ISO, was developing a seven-layer model standardizing the interconnection of computers without regard for their underlying internal structure. That bundled a set of specialized activities into a series of well-organized strata of individual functions. So logically, it was known as the Open Systems Interconnect model or OSI. That model was adopted as the conceptual framework of a worldwide distributed network architecture, which then became the internet."

Tom said, "That developmental history is an easy way to teach students to understand the basic protocols and layering concepts of data transmission. They need to see how the OSI's layering concepts break the transmission function into a distinct set of operational layers, each of which contains a standard protocol that is specifically designed to fulfill each layer's task. These protocol layers work together to enable an electronic signal at the lowest end of the process to be turned into an email message at the highest level. So, we should have the students map the transmission of a message through the various layers from signal to the eventual text. Each protocol has a well-defined task. Therefore, it is easy for us to describe what each layer is doing. For example, the delivery of the message is one task, and the management of the connection is another. Those two processes function in separate layers. So, we could devote one day to describing how the message delivery process works using the post office as an example and the next day to connection control using the process of actually addressing the letter."

Lucy said, pleased, "That was an excellent section, guys. I can see exactly how to teach those three topics. It's handy that we can bundle them together into a single part of the course. But what in the world do we do about High-performance computing and Hypervisors and cloud computing? The Doc laughed and said, "That's easy. We ignore them. The CSEC is meant to include every potential topic in a knowledge area, but that doesn't mean you have to teach it at every level in the educational process. For example, high-performance computing aggregates resources to accomplish a given task. That is a professional concern that would probably be appropriate in grad school and is certainly important in professional computing. But it is far too advanced to introduce in a secondary school.

Furthermore, it might lead to confusion since the technology is complex and the solution is convoluted, which could also be said of hypervisors. They are virtual machine implementations to facilitate all kinds of "As a Service" implementations such as infrastructure as a service (IaaS), Software as a Service (SaaS), or Platform as a Service (PaaS). One of the most popular and widespread applications of hypervisor technology is cloud computing, a powerful technology that people going into the field will have to master. But it is unrealistic to think that high school students are ready to dive into cloud architectures. The best we can do is introduce the concept of virtuality in both cases and help the students understand that there are such things as virtual machines.

Tom said, "How do we deal with vulnerabilities then? That's the last item in this category." The Doc said, "Well, logically, there are two broad categories of network vulnerabilities – malicious code and attacks. Malicious code is always a problem. However, commercial screening products safeguard against the more common examples. So, it should be sufficient to demonstrate how a few of the most popular automated virus checkers like McAfee and Norton work. On the other hand, we should discuss attacks completely because there are so many different ways a network can be attacked."

Lucy said, "So what does that mean in practical terms?" The Doc said, "The network attack surface constitutes all possible access points. At the same time, vulnerabilities constitute all of the feasible ways to exploit those access points. That includes user input fields, network protocols themselves, any accessible interface, and any application or service running on the network."

Lucy said skeptically, "Those can be pretty much anything, Doc. There's no way of keeping track of that." Before the Doc could answer him, Tom said, "That isn't true, Lucy. Suppose we concentrate the discussion on the known vulnerabilities. In that case, there is a database at *CWE – Common Weakness Enumeration (mitre.org)* that lists every potential weakness that has been identified so far, and if we ask the students to explore how those vulnerabilities can be exploited, all we have to do is send them to a companion database which is at *CAPEC – Common Attack Pattern Enumeration and Classification (CAPEC) (mitre. org)*. There, they can look up all the background information on how all known attacks are carried out. So, if we want our students to learn about specific network vulnerabilities, we could have them pick one of the most common ones from the SANS top-25 list at *Top 25 Software Errors | SANS Institute* and then report on what the database has to say about it. Of course, the students might not understand all of the professional jargon recorded about that vulnerability, but it would give them familiarity with how to find out about network vulnerabilities from the industry's common reference." The Doc said delightedly, "That's right, Tom!! You've clearly researched on your own."

## EXERCISE

### THE DAWN OF THE NET

Watch the short video called "The Dawn of the Net – How the Internet works" through the following website: https://www.youtube.com/watch?v=hymzoUpM0K0. After listening to the video, identify three security vulnerabilities that might exist when using the internet and the World Wide Web as part of a distributed architecture.

Topic Five: Building a Network

Tom said, "More importantly, the next CSEC knowledge area seems to cover things that are too far down in the machine for high school. For example, we mention concepts like forwarding, routing, and switches in our networking class. They're a basic part of any network. But we don't detail how to implement any of those things. We just define their purpose and tell the students why those functions are important. It takes up less than a full hour in one class."

The Doc said, "I agree, Tom... Realistically, the details of how those things operate in practice is a professional concern, which is best introduced in an engineering school. But we DO have to start somewhere in teaching the fundamental building blocks of networking."

The Doc stopped and added, "Your students DO need to know about the basic concepts that a network embodies and how they relate to each other. Therefore, the network architecture topic is where you present and clarify ALL of the top-level concepts that underlie connectivity and the hardware devices, network protocols, and transmission modes. In that respect, then, this section is where we give our students a comprehensive grasp of the basic elements of the data communication process."

Lucy said, "Noble words Doc but specifically, what do we concentrate on here?" The Doc chuckled fondly and said, "You're always practical, Lucy." Then he added, "Seriously though, the standard elements of network architecture consist of communications hardware, including the cables and devices that facilitate the transfer. It also includes the physical layout, which we call a topology, and the characteristics of the physical and wireless connectors. In addition, there's the dedicated software functionality and protocols that are needed to move the data from point to point. All of that is part of the tangible network architecture area."

Lucy was looking at the CSEC. She said, "There are seven topics associated with this knowledge unit:

1. *General concepts*: the primary network characteristics as represented in the topologies.
2. *Common architectures*: this purportedly covers the IEEE 802 network architecture. That's a professional concern – right? I don't see it as part of a secondary curriculum.

3. *Forwarding*: this is about packet forwarding. It depends too much on complex algorithms, which is not anything high school kids should be taught.
4. *Routing*: routing systems.
5. *Switching/Bridging*: involves using standardized behavioral algorithms, which is also over the heads of secondary students.
6. *Emerging trends*: which looks at developing technologies and their impact." Lucy paused and said thoughtfully, "I think we ought to cover that."
7. *Virtualization and virtual hypervisor architecture*: is way out of bounds for a high school curriculum.

Tom said, "That just leaves two things in this knowledge area that might apply at the high school level, General Concepts and Emerging trends – right, Doc?" The Doc said delightedly, "You two are getting the hang of this. The fact is that network architecture is a very deep and complex area of inquiry. We need to teach the fundamentals. But much of the actual implementation concerns dive down to a level of detail that is more realistically considered in the professional domain. So, much of the network implementation details belong at the graduate or professional level, not in a high school classroom. Since our purpose in secondary education is to teach the essential concepts that will be built on as the student's understanding develops through the later stages in the process, I think we need to just concentrate on the foundation."

Lucy said, "So we should introduce and explain the architectural standards, forwarding, routing, switching, and bridging and hypervisors and why those are all important. But we should leave it at that, not venture into the implementation details." The Doc said appreciatively, "I think that makes good practical sense. The body of knowledge has to be inclusive. So logically, there will be parts that simply don't apply at a given level. Our challenge here is to teach the things the students need to know to take the next step up the ladder, which means that we have to decide what doesn't fit in a high school curriculum. In that respect, we draw the line at topics that require more advanced knowledge or professional expertise to master."

Tom said, "According to the CSEC, the general concepts topic is embodied through the various commonly accepted topologies and their transmission characteristics. Even my students know those standard topology arrangements: star, bus, ring, and mesh. So we need to explain what those look like and ask the students to discuss the advantages of one topology over another in supporting a LAN, or a WAN." The Doc said, "Yes, the issues in topology are related to performance. If you can get your students to appreciate how each of these standard arrangements serves a particular purpose performance-wise, that is all they need to know. One way to do that is to have a competition where you break the class into four groups and have each group make a sales pitch for their topology. That should help them understand how to make practical tradeoffs and be fun simultaneously."

Lucy said, "Once we do that, we can have a teaching section where we define what an IEEE 802 standard network architecture is and its role in physical media access control. We can also discuss the basic steps involved in routing and forwarding. We can do it in the same context with the postal addresses that we used to illustrate internet packet delivery. The actual calculation of the delivery path takes place in the hardware. But we avoid talking about the routing algorithms and forwarding tables that ensure the optimum delivery path. That's something that belongs later in the education process. Still, the students must understand the basic process and reason for passing messages from node to node in a network. We should also avoid getting into the operational details of switching and bridging because that would force us to discuss Ethernet's mechanics. Finally, we need to stay away from virtual hypervisor architecture since the concept of abstract machines belongs much later in the learning process."

Tom said, "That's what we agreed on, Lucy. All of those topics are important. But they are on the other side of the line we've drawn." Lucy said, "Well, that just leaves emerging trends. What specifically does that entail?" The Doc said, "Unfortunately, I can't tell you anything concrete because that topic intends to make students aware that developing technologies and their changes are important. But since these technologies are emerging, there isn't any way that you can draw up a list of things that have yet to happen."

Tom read the document, and he added, "As an example, the CSEC suggests innovations like centralized network management are appropriate. That emerging technology is enabled by a concept called SDN, which allows the hardware parts of the network to be managed independently from the routing and forwarding elements. Nevertheless, that perfectly illustrates something too complex for high school kids to understand. So, the easiest way to introduce an emerging concepts section into our teaching would be to simply have the students cruise the internet to identify what they think is an important new concept and then write a term paper explaining why." Lucy said, "That makes sense, Tom. But what you seem to be telling us is that the emerging trends area is just a placeholder that says. 'If anything new or innovative comes up, you ought to discuss it' otherwise, we should just pass it on to the next CSEC topic, implementation."

## EXERCISE

### THE FUTURE IS NOW!

We often think about network architecture as connecting devices that provide communication capability. But what about the connection of the unconnected? The Internet of Things (IoT) is an up-and-coming technology in networking. Browse some sites on the internet and identify three types of communication within your own home that, within the next five years, could potentially take advantage of IoT technology.

### Topic Six: The Bits and Pieces of Network Operation

Tom, who was still reading the CSEC, said, "This knowledge unit seems to cover the topics that allow networks to function properly. In some respects, it serves as a summary of all the explicit content that preceded it in the Distributed Network topic area. The difference is that these topics are the pragmatic considerations associated with data transmission: (1) *IEEE 802/ISO standards*: which we just bypassed in that section. Still, Ethernet is so ubiquitous, and its standards are so critical to the physical connection process that this needs to be explained in a little more detail. Along with that first topic, we also have (2) *TCP/IP* and the *IETF*. Those are the standard transmission concepts, and the IETF is the organization that enables the internet, which deserves some high-level discussion. Then finally, there is something about (3) *Practical integration protocols*. The details of that topic are too advanced for high school. But the idea of the process of actively fitting the elements of the network together through programming has to have some discussion. And finally, there is the consideration of (4) *Vulnerabilities and example exploits*. In some ways, this is a rehash of the 'vulnerabilities' topic under distributed systems. We need to provide specific examples of the types of attacks on network equipment."

Lucy said coolly, "I'll take your word for that, Tom." She was not impressed by the usefulness of anything in this topic area. She turned to the Doc and said, "So Doc, what are the IEEE 802 standards? The whole thing sounds like a waste of time at the secondary level, but maybe you can convince me otherwise." The Doc laughed and said, "They may be more interesting to the nerd population, Lucy. But the IEEE 802 standards DO define all of the rules for wireless and wired local area network communication at the physical level, meaning they standardize and thus unify anything you can see and touch that transmits data. IEEE aimed to create a series of professional standards to ensure network hardware safety, predictability, and usability. That's the purpose of the 802 standards. They define the common basis for connecting various networks so that disparate products can talk to one another. The only thing you need for your students to understand is that it would be impossible to transmit information between various manufacturers' equipment if the 802 standards didn't exist." Tom said, "So we just need to emphasize the communication problem that the 802 series addresses, ensuring that the myriad of commercial networking products is compatible, right? We don't need to get into how that's done." The Doc said, "Yes, this is the point in the education process where it's important for high school students to understand the vital role standardization plays in ensuring our modern global communication system. Without standards, nobody could talk to anybody else. I know that's true because I'm from the era before standards, and we were all stranded on our little islands by our choice of manufacturers. This brings us to the ultimate interconnected network, the internet."

Tom said, "We learned in the B-School that the Internet Engineering Task Force, the IETF, regulates the internet. But here, the CSEC is concentrating on the Internet protocol suite, TCP/IP." The Doc said, "That's right, Tom. The IETF has served as the definitive governing body for the internet since 1993. It was chartered as a corporation to develop and promulgate standards for the internet, and it was one of the key contributors to its development. The standards it oversees were originally developed by the Defense Advanced Research Projects Administration (DARPA) and known as the Transmission Control Protocol/Internet Protocol, or TCP/IP. TCP/IP defines the underlying structure of the Internet, and it describes the process by which data is encapsulated into packets, addressed and transmitted, through the internet's routing, and receiving functions."

Lucy said, "Well, that sounds simple enough. All we have to do is present the history and the current work of the IETF and ensure that the students understand the basics of packet transmission. I think that my junior high students could even do that since it's a simple matter of memorizing what a packet looks like and how it's routed. But what in the world is the next item, *Practical Integration?*"

The Doc said, "We've talked a lot about hardware architecture and the data transmission concepts that enable networks. But we haven't focused on the issues associated with how networks are assembled from the basic building blocks of endpoints, routers, switches, and protocols. Network developers must ensure that diverse and not necessarily compatible technologies work together. So, the purpose of this topic is to discuss interoperability. That means that the students have to be taught that hardware devices can only communicate if their developer provides a means for doing so. That usually involves installing some intermediary translator device or program to bridge the difference between two different devices."

Lucy was starting to see the problem presented by having to wire a bunch of unrelated parts into a single seamless system. She said emphatically, "Now THAT's not a trivial process. So, we need to focus on the problem of translation. One way to do that would be to challenge the students to find a way for a French speaker and a German speaker to communicate. It might be through translation; it might be through some gadget that converts one person's words into the other person's language. But the students need to understand that compatibility is an absolute requirement in data transmission, and it has to be established by something tangible."

Tom looked at the next topic, Vulnerabilities, and said, "This looks pretty redundant to me. We just talked about vulnerabilities in the Distributed Systems section. How is this different?" The Doc said, "It probably isn't for our purposes. The whole point of the network defense operation is to stay on top of vulnerabilities. In practical terms, that means that vulnerabilities must be identified and either patched or fixed as part of the day-to-day operation of the system." Lucy stated the obvious. She said, "So what? I don't see anything to teach here except a laundry list of things that might go wrong. How is that useful?"

The Doc laughed and said, "Vulnerabilities can be classified. You can at least make the students aware of those types." Tom said skeptically, "Such as?" The Doc said, "Well, there are the *backdoor* attacks. That's any concealed way to bypass normal authentication or security controls. Backdoors are either intentional, or as in many cases, accidental. Then there is *spoofing* which is a situation where one person or program successfully masquerades as another. There's also *tampering*, where data or capabilities are changed. Finally, there are the *social engineering* attacks like phishing. Phishing is a widespread way to obtain sensitive information, and it is a purely behavioral attack typically carried out by email spoofing or instant messaging. All these things are something that the student has to be aware of, so it would be valuable if you at least reviewed what each type of attack is and what can be done to counter them."

## EXERCISE

### DEFEND THE CROWN

Download from Apple Store or Google Play the game "Defend the Crown." In the game, Cyber ninjas are trying to raid your castle and steal your valuable secrets! You must stop them at all costs when you play *Defend the Crown*. As you work through three challenging stages and 18 levels, identify how the game has increased your knowledge of different cyber-attack categories.

Top Seven: The Practical Considerations of Building a Network

Tom looked at the CSEC as he said, "I think I see a trend emerging. We seem to be following the OSI model from bottom to top. So the previous two topics looked at distributed systems from the physical and data link levels, that was where the IEEE 802 standards came in, and then we looked at the network and transport level, which was TCP/IP. This final topic focuses on teaching students about the top levels in the OSI hierarchy, the ones where the applications operate. Consequently, this section explores the standard ideas and methods associated with the networking process as normal people would experience it."

The Doc said, "Yes, of course, the ability for a disparate set of distributed software applications to work together through a central server is where the real usefulness of computers lies, and that's what the CSEC is concentrating on here."

Lucy said, "Let me get this straight. I think you just said that the past two topic areas dealt with physical and data communication concepts. This section deals with how a wide range of different applications, which sit on top of the prior two levels, interact." The Doc said approvingly, "Couldn't have said it better! This topic area focuses on the traditional network configuration issues. So, in many respects, this is the area that most frequently appears in a networking course. I'm sure Tom already talks about:

1. *Concept of a service* – which is a top-level look at the various types of network services.
2. *Service models* – which is where the students learn about the classic types of network configurations such as client-server and peer-to-peer.
3. *Service protocols* – which are the various standard ways that components and applications are connected to each other.
4. *Common service communication architectures topic area* – which looks at each specific network service and how the relevant protocols are implemented.

That is about as far as you go in a high school classroom because:

5. *Service virtualization* topic area focuses on emulation which really belongs at the college level.

6. *Vulnerabilities_and_example_exploits* topic that was in the conclusion of the other two sections. Except for this time we are talking about the vulnerabilities of client-server and peer-to-peer services, which is a lot more immediate and familiar to the average person."

Lucy said, "So the first topic is the concept of a service. Explain that Doc and tell me why we ought to be teaching it." The Doc said, "As the name implies, this topic overviews the commonly understood services that validate the use of a computer. In effect, this is the place where you help the students understand what a networked application is and how it engages users, other devices, or maybe even another network in the practical process of satisfying some generic human purpose. Because those purposes can be anything that a network can conceivably do, you are essentially talking about whatever takes place in the world of computing."

Lucy said, "So how do we teach this? There is no way you could ask the students to get their minds around something that's so fuzzy. After all, we're talking about the entire world of applications. There are just too many different things involved, and it would be like trying to teach them everything about the insect world." The Doc said, "Obviously, you're right. The idea of distributing application services across a network DOES include most things we do in the modern world. So instead, we need to focus on helping our students understand the relatively few models used to enable application sharing. The goal of distributing specific services to a wide range of clients via a shared connection is the single justification for a network operation. So, if the students understand the general concepts that enable distributing applications and data by means of a common source, they will have mastered the single overall goal of a network."

Tom said, "I guess the concept of sharing can be illustrated by discussing the standard models, like client-server, or peer-to-peer" The Doc said approvingly, "Absolutely Tom! The oldest and probably the best example of sharing is a client-server architecture. As you know, the concept goes back to the beginning of the PC revolution. It was a way of 'distributing' the processing load across more than one personal computer. In its simplest form, the client simply initiates a connection that the server responds to. However, in modern computing the connection process can entail everything from DNS architecture and the internet, all the way down to the client-server interactions of any humble three-node local area network."

Tom added, "But, there still have to be mechanisms for establishing the connections and managing the traffic in a client-server relationship. Not coincidentally, that happens to be the next topic – service protocols." The Doc said, "Yes, the network service protocols actually establish the connection between the various clients and the server. But, the connection process has to take place at the basic operating system level in each of those devices. So, the mechanics of doing that are not something you'd want to introduce at the high school level. But your students DO need to know about APIs."

Lucy said, "Oh boy! More acronyms!!" The Doc said, laughing, "An Application Programming Interface, or API, is a little bridging program that every client-side application runs when it wants to access a server resident service. In that respect then, APIs might be considered to be the bridges that make client and server communication possible."

Lucy said, "How do you teach something like that?" The Doc said, "Well basically, an API is nothing more than a piece of code that helps two different software programs exchange data with each other. So the approach that we utilized before of having a translator communicate back and forth between two different people illustrates the function of APIs."

Lucy said, "Okay, I see that Doc. It's funny, you know. A lot of those intimidating acronyms actually describe a very simple action. I suppose the term 'translator' covers too much territory but why can't we just call an API what it is – a connector." Both Tom and the Doc laughed. Tom said, "I get your point, Lucy. But since they're active, that understates the role of APIs in client server processing, and since connectors are everywhere in a network, it won't narrow things down very much."

The Doc said, "Our task is to ensure all of the basic concepts of distributed processing are mastered before the students begin to dive into the details of how to accomplish the actual process. This normally takes place at the college level. Hence, we are building an essential base of understanding per-se, and there is no better illustration of that process than the next item, which is common service communication architectures."

Lucy threw up her hands in disgust and said, "I understand all of those words, yet I don't have the slightest idea what you're talking about."

Tom said curiously, "I agree. What ARE you talking about, Doc?" The Doc chuckled and said, "By definition, a common service is one and only one item of functionality, which can be remotely accessed and used in a network. At its most basic, a network is nothing more than a dedicated communication technology that facilitates interchanges between a given set of functions. Connecting disparate functions is fundamentally what a network does. So, we need our students to understand that at their most basic level, all networks share one common purpose." Like a light bulb had gone on in his head, Tom said, "And THAT is also why we are leaving service virtualization out of the curriculum, right? Virtualization adds to the capabilities of a network. But it does it by emulating those basic services. So, virtualization might be relevant in the study of cloud and service-oriented architectures. But it isn't integral to the basic networking concept."

Lucy said, "What about vulnerabilities then?" Tom said, "Just like in the other two sections, the vulnerability of client-server and peer-to-peer networks is a critical topic. But in this case, it is more a case of listing the most frequent forms of attack and exploitation. We can use the same sources for the physical and data communications topic areas to illustrate this. The best of those is the Mitre Adversary Attack and Tactics database at *MITRE ATT&CK®*. In fact, it might be a good idea to present all three of the vulnerability areas as a single unit using those resources since they normally apply to all three aspects of distributed system communication."

## EXERCISE

### GAMERS BEWARE!

One common use of client/server networking are the multi-user games we play every day, such as: War Thunder, Valorant, Among Us, Destiny 2, Apex Legends, and Fortnite. Each player acts as a client, while a server serves as a connection between them. Browse the internet for recent attacks that have been targeted toward multi-user games, and identify three things that you can do to protect yourself from those attacks.

### Top Eight: Network Defense

Lucy said wearily, "It's been a long day and this last topic looks like it might go on forever." The Doc said, "Not necessarily. Network defense activities fall into categories. So, like we did with Data Security, we can factor that laundry list into three categories based on their basic purpose. The only problem is that due to their operational focus, these topics only reflect the approaches we currently know about. So, although there are 13 subtopics in this last section, they can be factored into four instructional categories: (1) countermeasures, (2) defensive concepts, (3) policy and procedure, and (4) real-world methods. For instance, *network hardening* describes the standard approach to network protection. It simply requires the students to know what the current countermeasure thinking is. It's the same with *Firewalls and virtual private networks*. Those are the concepts that guide the creation of controlled access to a network. All the students would need to learn to master the countermeasures category are the common principles for ensuring against unauthorized access, like the basic authentication and authorization measures." Tom said, "Those are pretty elementary topics. We could cover firewalls in an hour on any given Monday. So, network hardening is just a case of memorizing a list of access control methods."

The Doc said, "Excellent, Tom, you're seeing this topic area for what it is, which is nothing more than the most current strategies for ensuring the confidentiality, integrity, and availability of data in a network. It's the same for the next category, defensive concepts. That category involves a bunch of evergreen principles that have been part of defensive thinking since the dawn of time. For instance, *defense in depth* is the idea of creating a series of progressively more robust defenses in order to force an adversary to expend increasingly greater effort to breach a perimeter. That same concept was an integral part of the design of medieval castles. Same with honeypots and *honeynets*. Those old-fashioned approaches create a vulnerable network for the purpose of intelligence gathering. But normal people would see it as baiting a trap." Lucy said astonished, "Wow!! It's THAT simple!!"

Tom, who was a B-School grad, said enthusiastically. "I see it now. The next category is just a series of the common managerial things that a student would need to be aware of like the need for *policy development and enforcement for a network* and the need to convert those policies into explicit real-world *operational procedures* that dictate how you plan the operation of that particular network. The process of turning organizational purposes into a set of concrete day-to-day actions is a relatively high-level activity that we study in our Introduction to Business class in the eleventh grade. All we would have to do is revisit the discussion when we get to this topic here, because it's the exact same thing."

The Doc said, "And that carries over into the last category, which is the proactive methods you employ for vulnerability detection and mitigation. The most obvious of those is penetration testing, but there are also the various types of inspections and tests that you undertake to identify prospective vulnerabilities in the network operation. There are so many ways to do that that you couldn't possibly cover all of them in detail. But you could pull a few pen-testing examples off the internet and have your students look at them."

Lucy said, "What are you talking about Doc?" The Doc said, "You really only need to show them some of the top examples of how to pen-test. There are plenty up there. In fact, the hard part will be deciding which one of the hundreds of thousands posted on YouTube you will use. You wouldn't be teaching pen-testing per-se. But your students DO need to know what these processes look like before they can dive down into the details of how to execute them."

Lucy said, "Is that what you're talking about when you say our role is to build a strong foundation?" The Doc said, "Absolutely!! Your students shouldn't get into zero knowledge exploits and reverse engineering in the tenth grade." Then he paused and said speculatively, "Although a few of the weirder ones might try. But when they get to college, everybody who is entering the field of cybersecurity studies ought to be aware of the principle of identifying vulnerabilities by attacking the system. So the first critical condition for studying cyberdefense is that the students know what common cyber defense tactics are. That's what you're providing for them here."

Lucy said, "Is that it, Doc, we just have to show them a few videos? It doesn't stop there, does it?" The Doc said, "Unfortunately not. There are a number of purely technical mechanisms like network monitors and traffic analyzers that the network's operational staff use to keep track of what's going on, on the network – or to do content filtering.

You should mention those and show how they work in principle. But you should really leave the technical details of how current professional defense in depth is implemented, such as proxy servers, and automated threat hunting tools and artificial intelligence to later college courses or when your students get into the profession. That's the smart thing to do since the universe of products is continuously changing and thus, whatever a student learns about in high school will no-doubt be outmoded by the time they get into the workforce. Our goal here is to focus on the underlying purpose of these gadgets. That will never change."

### EXERCISE

### CYBER THREAT DEFENDER

Browse to the webpage https://cias.utsa.edu/ctd_cards.php. Download the Windows or Mac version of Cyber Threat Defender, and then play the game. Cyber Threat Defender is a PC- or Mac-based game that allows you to play against the computer. It plays a lot like a regular card game but it creates a competitive experience that will teach you how to build defense strategies with online cards and implement strategies aimed at expanding and protecting your network. After playing the game, identify how that experience has enhanced your understanding of network defense.

Tom said, relieved, "Wow! That wasn't as hard as it looked." Lucy said, "You know – that's what I hate about any topic area that has a title that's the same as the entire knowledge area. I mean, network defense is the whole point of the Connection Security function – isn't it? So, why stick a category on the end of these recommendations that invokes a laundry list of concepts that more-or-less cover the same topics we just discussed?"

The Doc said, "I see what you're talking about; Lucy and I agree. But I guess that the people who developed the CSEC wanted to conclude this vitally important knowledge area with a straightforward statement about the general actions required to do connection security properly. So, they essentially summarized all of the salient topics by listing the practical concepts associated with their application. So, it's a way to highlight them for anybody thinking about the basics of the network security design and operation area."

Lucy was in the middle of helping Tom, and the Doc gather up the empty donut boxes as she said, "This section may have been a long trudge, but I DO agree that it is important to have a complete catalog of the things that you'd need to know if you want to assure a network. Nonetheless, there are definitely a lot of things in this area of knowledge." As he was going out the door Tom said, "The next section is System Security and maybe it will be fewer things to get through. I'll see you guys tomorrow."

# 6

# SYSTEM SECURITY

## Assembling the Parts into a Useful Whole

The Three Musketeers met the next day. They knew they were on a roll and wanted to finish the work. So again, Lucy brought the Doc's donuts, and this time the Doc got the coffee. It was a hot day, and all three were in t-shirts and shorts. But the Doc was wearing a wild pair of Bermuda Shorts with suspenders and knee socks. He looked like he'd dropped out of a 1950s time-warp. Lucy suppressed a laugh as she said, "You look sporty today." The Doc said, "Why, thank you, Lucy. I wanted to show you whipper-snappers what real fashion looks like."

Tom said, grinning, "Well then, maybe you can also tell us how to approach this area since it looks like your outfit, made up from the pieces-and-parts of all of the others." The Doc missed the snark in Tom's comment entirely as he said, "That's very astute, Tom. In many respects, the system security knowledge area is the glue that binds the software security, component security, and connection security knowledge areas together. In effect, system security is the place where the holistic concepts that ensure both general purpose and special purpose computer systems come together into a single unified model."

Lucy said eyebrows raised, "General purpose? More terminology??!" The Doc laughed and said, "Yes – a general-purpose system is what most people are talking about when they use the term 'computer.' Of course, it applies to every device that runs a conventional operating system. But your students also have to be aware that special-purpose systems are just as important and, in some respects, even more critical."

Lucy said, "Okay, wise one, what's the difference between general purpose and special purpose, and why should I care?" The Doc laughed again and said, "General purpose computers are on everybody's radar because they are a part of their daily lives. Those are

DOI: 10.1201/9781003187172-6

**Figure 6.1**   Tom and Lucy get a good laugh about the Doc's outfit.

the desktops, laptops, tablets, and smartphones that everybody uses. Those devices all execute a wide and diverse range of commercial applications."

Tom piped up with, "Wouldn't that make general-purpose systems more likely to be exploited? Since they will only be as secure as the applications they run, and most applications have flaws in them?" The Doc said "That's right, Tom. And that's the reason why general-purpose assurance practices tend to be synonymous with what we call cybersecurity."

The Doc added, "But there are also systems that carry out only one pre-programmed action, such as controlling a robotic device, regulating a process, or even banking like an ATM." Tom said, "I hadn't thought of that. But doesn't their one purpose make them easier to protect? So you don't have to worry about anything but the threats to that specific purpose."

The Doc said, "In many respects, that is correct. However, special-purpose systems don't need to be protected from the wide spectrum of potential compromises like their more versatile brethren. That is because single-purpose computers only do one thing. Consequently, we can eliminate many potential compromises and only concentrate on what we know would impact that one specific function."

Then he added warningly, "Still, single-purpose systems underlie our critical infrastructure. So, they are like the insect world, meaning they're everywhere, mainly invisible unless you look carefully. But because their services have made our society what it is today, any compromise of a single-purpose computer system, like the one that controls our electrical grid, could be disastrous. Thus, the stakes are higher with single-purpose systems."

Tom said, "I don't understand that last statement?" The Doc said, "Think about it, Tom. Everything we do in our modern world is enabled by programmed logic. For instance, there isn't a little man in a box controlling how electricity is distributed to your home. That's all handled by pre-programmed logic pieces embedded in the electrical grid. If those are ever compromised, all of the lights go off permanently. That's why system security has to address both general purpose and specialized systems."

The Doc added, "It should be clear by now that any system is complex. Hence, the only way to guarantee effective protection is to employ the right countermeasures. As a result, we need to have a concrete set of organizing principles to ensure that all the diverse elements of any solution are merged into a single unified scheme."

The adversary will exploit every gap. So, I can see why we need completeness. However, cyber-attacks are diverse and often unique, and the inter-dependencies that underlie large computer systems are wide-ranging and unpredictable.

The Doc said, "I agree with your statement, but the principles you use to fashion a logical and complete cybersecurity response are no different from those you'd use to create any complex structure. Whether it's your home computer network or Amazon's package distribution system, we need to consider a few basic things we need to consider. Those are the same principles that underlie system thinking and those generic concepts are what's contained in the system security knowledge area."

Lucy, who had been looking increasingly frustrated with the fuzziness of the discussion, said, "Can you restate what you just said in English? I'm a junior high school teacher, not a system theorist." The Doc laughed and said, "You're right, Lucy. We were wandering into blue sky territory. But the entire area of system theory is just so darn interesting." Lucy muttered under her breath, "Maybe for some people."

The Doc said, warming to the question, "A system is any combination of interdependent parts that have been arrayed into a unitary whole for some particular purpose. That system itself is synergistic because its overall impact is greater than the sum of the effect of the individual parts. But each part of that whole has its specific function."

The Doc added, "Systems are *dynamic* because changing one element will affect all other elements. However, they are also *emergent* because there is always the need to evolve in form and function as changes in the environment influence them. These are the principles we're talking about."

Tom said, "I can see that. You're saying that you have to continue to fully understand how a system is built, how the parts interact, and the environment to secure it properly. That's just critical thinking which is a process that we start to teach students in the fifth grade."

The Doc said, "That's correct, Tom; the systems security area topics comprise all of the activities you would typically have to carry out to ensure a complete, correct, and efficient solution. Those things are classic system engineering and management concepts, which have traditionally motivated information technology thinking for decades.

> **System Thinking** describes the common principles that underlie the creation of holistic systems.
>
> **System Management** looks at how consistent oversight over a system is established.
>
> **System Access** are the basic cybersecurity access control methods.
>
> **System Control** encompasses the governance part of the security solution.
>
> **System Retirement** is the standard method for securely disposing of a system and its data.
>
> **System Testing** is the process of validating and verifying the correctness of the solution.
>
> **Common System Architectures** is the classic end piece where prominent examples are discussed."

## Topic One: Thinking Systematically

Lucy said, "That's a lot of pieces and parts, but I can see that they are just the logical steps in building a system. So let's get started. What do you think they mean by *system thinking*, Doc?" The Doc said,

"As both of you have pointed out, this area's real title ought to be 'critical thinking.' The system approach is essentially any structured method people employ to analyze a complex situation. It's the classic problem-solving technique of breaking something down into its more understandable parts and then describing what those parts are and how they interact."

The Doc stopped and emphasized, "In essence, the topics contained in the system thinking area involve a classification and analysis process. You always approach the problem the same way. First, you divide the overall entity into its constituent elements. Then you develop a complete and correct set of control behaviors to ensure that every known aspect of threat and vulnerability has been addressed. In that respect, system thinking is holistic. It seeks to find and address every potential avenue that an adversary can exploit to compromise a given entity's components, or the system itself." Then the Doc stopped and added, "Of course, system thinking also has to consider the environmental influences." Lucy said, sounding puzzled, "Environment? What does the environment have to do with it?"

Tom understood what the Doc was saying. He said, "Think about it, Lucy. All entities are influenced by the environment in which they exist. For instance, your car would have to deal with different factors if it were in the Daytona 500 rather than sitting in your driveway. So, the particular actions would have to be tailored to the situation, while the aspect of the basic car is the same. Understanding the interaction with the environment is as much a part of system thinking as analyzing the interrelationship of the components."

Lucy said, "Yes, I see that. But how does system thinking relate to what we teach our students? I mean, the topic is theoretical, not practical." The Doc said, "System thinking involves creative problem-solving, which your students ought to find interesting. However, it requires people to develop practical responses to real-world conditions. For instance, you could ask one team to put together a plan to protect a general-purpose computer system from every logical form of attack and have the other team think of every conceivable way to attack it."

Tom said, "How would we do that, though? Wouldn't we have to have some way to identify and evaluate those threats to make plans to mitigate them?" The Doc said, "That's right, Tom, which is why you could also teach them threat modeling to think through the details of the problem graphically." Lucy said, "What's a threat model?" The Doc laughed and said. "Threat modeling is any structured graphic approach that you use to think through the structure of a system."

Lucy said, "Seriously!! How do you do that? I mean, what's the purpose?" The Doc said, "The aim of the modeling is to describe how the system operates so you can identify all potential threats and weaknesses. The commonly used methods are graphic, like *data flow diagrams, or UML drawings* that identify how data flows into a system and is processed and stored. A data flow or a UML diagram identifies the input data to a system, how and where it is entered, the processing that ensues, and finally where the data is stored."

Lucy said, "Practically speaking, how do you accomplish that?" The Doc said, "Most of it is a matter of drawing up the actual processing steps of the system. It's also a bit of a creative exercise in that you try to think of potential points of compromise along the way – for every aspect of data entry, processing, and storage. The aim is to identify the places in the operation where a specific attack might succeed."

Tom said, "I get it!! We could have the students develop creative 'what if' suppositions about the processing using data flow diagrams. They could identify things that could go wrong as they work through the input and storage processes. That way the students could think through the likely threats step by step. It would allow them to identify and describe the dependencies and interrelationships among the various system functions. For example, how does the input screen relate to eventual storage, and how could that be compromised?"

The Doc said approvingly, "That's excellent, Tom. But, of course, you always have to use three fundamental qualities to judge whether a system is secure. Those are the relative levels of *confidentiality, integrity,* and *availability* of the information. So, you need to ensure that the system maintains all three essentials in proper balance, which means that the students could demonstrate that their solution will ensure these qualities."

He added, "Thus, the last part of system thinking is documenting the logic of your assurance scheme. You have to prove that the system is protected against all credible threats. But you also have to ensure that the controls themselves achieve the desired levels of confidentiality and integrity in light of the need to make information available.

So besides simply developing an assurance scheme, your students also need to have a concrete plan to ensure that the assurance is properly balanced and effective in a real-world application. They can do that on a piece of paper using modeling."

## EXERCISE

## ELEVATION OF PRIVILEGE

The game Elevation of Privilege is a popular, fun, and easy way to create a system thinking mindset by playing a game that reinforces the concepts of threat modeling. Begin by browsing the website: https://www.microsoft.com/en-us/download/details.aspx?id=20303 and click the "Download" button to download the five files available for the game. After downloading, read through the instructions and whitepaper before unzipping the EOP native files. Once the game is installed on your computer, form 3–6 players' teams. After having the gaming experience, what did you learn about system thinking and the importance of threat modeling?

### Topic Two: Managing What You Create

Tom said, "Okay, so what do we do with system management? That seems fuzzier?" The Doc said, "All systems have a purpose, which is achieved by consistently executing a pre-planned set of program functions. System managers oversee the day-to-day execution of those functions."

Tom said, "So let me get this straight. If system thinking focuses on holistic solutions, then system management aims to ensure the proper implementation of that thinking, right?" The Doc said, "That's right, Tom. System management performs a diverse set of tasks. But it's always just the role that converts system thinking into a real-world functioning system. That's probably why the CSEC presents the system management topic directly after the system thinking section."

The Doc added, from a security standpoint, "The system management topic area describes how security policy is established and enforced during the operational life cycle of the system." Lucy said, "Okay, so what exactly does policy setting involve?" The Doc said,

"As the name implies, the system management function needs to ensure the system's proper operation. Therefore, system management develops both the direction and the detailed work instructions that define the shape of the everyday operation. The outcome of the system management process is a rational set of procedures that are aimed at securing every relevant system asset or system service within the organization."

Lucy said, "That's still pretty vague, Doc. How, exactly, is that done? What are the specific things that system management is responsible for?" The Doc said, "System management is responsible for developing long-term policies that govern how the organization will operate. In the case of system security, those policies specifically define how each asset will be protected from the known threats in the operational environment."

Lucy said, "So, what are we talking about here, Doc? What are the actions required? We have to teach the students something." The Doc said, "System management ensures the reliable operation of a rational and substantive process. Done properly, a system management function will embody all of the requisite traits of completeness, correctness, and protection that are needed to maintain an effective enterprise-wide service."

Lucy was getting frustrated. She said, "That's a noble objective, Doc. But practically speaking, how is that accomplished?" The Doc laughed and said, "System management typically involves the routine operation and maintenance of a given system. The term that is used to describe that activity is 'sustainment.' Since the sustainment period will always represent the greatest investment of time and money, the system management <u>plan</u> is an extremely influential contributor to the overall goal of practical system security."

Tom was looking at the CSEC. He said to paraphrase this, and the system management area centers on policy development, which I assume is nothing more than the formal statements that dictate how the system will operate in the long term. Those policies are operationalized by procedures that specify the tasks undertaken to achieve policy goals.

Lucy said, "Well, that would be easy to teach. Just have the students make a list of best use policies and then provide detailed instructions about how those policies would be carried out. We could have them do it in teams and then critique the other team's policy and procedure recommendations to identify gaps." The Doc said, "That's excellent, Lucy. That is no different from how the system management process operates in the real world."

Tom, who was ever-the-nerd, added, "But since those procedures inevitably require automation, policy recommendations and criteria for firewalls and intrusion detection systems have to be. There are also the decisions associated with patching throughout the system life cycle. Then there is the system's retirement, including decommissioning at the useful life cycle end. Finally, there is the issue of maintaining effective documentation. That includes security logs and other tracking and operational details. So how do we deal with all of that?"

The Doc said, "As part of the overall exercise, Tom. Some of the procedural responses to policy requirements will be behavioral. But just as many will involve dictating the basic criteria for firewall decision-making and even placement of the firewalls within the architecture, for deciding what degree of sensitivity criteria will be programmed into the incident response system. The actual programming of that is easy. It's thinking through the best place to establish the boundaries for the automated response that's difficult. Consequently, as part of Lucy's exercise, the students would need to recommend the applicable criteria and sensitivity settings for the firewall and the intrusion detection system given a specific threat level and be prepared to defend those recommendations."

He added, "Since most of those pre-programmed criteria involve access to the asset, one of the overall roles of system management policy is to ensure sufficient access control." Lucy said, "Wouldn't that also include specifying how access control will be implemented for each system within the overall organization." The Doc said, "Excellent, Lucy. All systems are managed by some type of plan or ad-hoc criteria. Specifically, these criteria embody best practice advice about proper system security management and use. So there are organization-wide policies that guide the overall security process. But there are also targeted policies designed to explicitly mitigate each particular system's risks. Those targeted policies guide the assurance process for the individual system asset."

Tom added, "Since most of those procedures are automated, particularly access control, doesn't system administration also oversee policies for automation," The Doc said, "Excellent point Tom and the simple answer is, of course, they do. Firewalls and intrusion detection systems are primary examples of where automation policies will be required. Defense-in-depth designs use numerous firewalls and intrusion prevention or detection system (IDS/IPS), which are set up to protect a well-defined perimeter of the overall system. The policies specify where the various system assets will be placed within the overall defense-in-depth scheme and the defensive boundaries."

The Doc added, "That also applies to patching." Lucy said, "What's patching?" The Doc said, "Patching is a software assurance term. It refers to the lifecycle actions taken to maintain the security and integrity of the system software throughout its use. Gaps and defects appear over time. So, you need a policy for how to address them effectively. In simple terms, every individually identified vulnerability requires a risk management decision concerning whether, or how, it will be patched or otherwise mitigated."

Lucy said, "If it is case by case, how do you teach it?" The Doc said, "You don't teach decision-making. You teach students about the patching process and why you need it. So much of the actual change management is taught in undergraduate software engineering or business IT courses, but the actual patching work needs overall context. That is what you can provide here by teaching students what patching is and its general advantages and pitfalls."

Tom said, "Then patching is just part of the everyday operation of the system." The Doc said, "That's right, Tom. Patches address identified vulnerabilities and their release is coordinated by system management. But of course, some of the harm to the system might be the result of accidental misuse. So, consideration also must be paid to ensure ease of operation because the system itself isn't the point; it's the work it supports. Therefore, the ideal is to ensure a common understanding of the patching process right up to the inevitable decommissioning."

Lucy said, "What does decommissioning have to do with it?" Tom said, "Think about it. A decommissioned system might still contain residual data of value to any attacker. So, there have to be plans to ensure that the contents of old systems are sanitized." Lucy said, "How do you teach THAT?" Tom said, "All of this is done based on criteria and a schedule. But decommissioning is something that is better taught at more advanced levels. So, the only thing we should be doing is getting the students to understand why systems have to be decommissioned due to things like wear-and-tear or planned obsolescence and that they need to be sanitized when they are. Then, we can leave it to higher education and the profession to teach them the trade tricks."

Lucy said, "Thanks, I get that. So, all we have left is documentation. How is that important?" The Doc said, "Documentation makes the system and its security functionality visible to the world-at-large. It's anything from the best-use policy to the specification of requirements for the system security functions. It can be simple end-user awareness or something more technical, including security logs and other tracking and operational details. All documentation must be fully protected from loss or harm because much of it constitutes proof of compliance with any outside security laws and regulations."

Lucy said, "So, I assume our only role here would be to make students aware of the range of standard documentation items and their purpose? Maybe we could familiarize them with the compliance requirements for some of the better-known laws such as HIPAA." The Doc said, "That's an excellent idea, Lucy!! Since the actual documentation requirements are impossibly varied, we can't make them memorize a list. But we can make them aware of the importance of system documentation, and we can highlight that by discussing practical requirements using laws or regulations."

### EXERCISE

### LAY DOWN THE LAW

Many federal, state, and local laws and regulations drive what policies must be in place to provide standardized system security practices. Browse the internet to identify two laws or rules that directly affect you. Then, write a paragraph about what you found, and describe a system or management policy you might implement to be in conformance.

Topic Three: Controlling Access

Lucy said, "So the next topic area is system access. I thought we covered access control in data security?" The Doc said, "We did; however, this topic is a different matter. It's the critical issue of controlling access to system <u>use</u>, not its data." Tom asked, "Isn't this access control more operationally oriented. It's about making certain that entities who use the system are properly authorized to do so."

The Doc said, "That's right! System access control involves deciding who you can allow inside the system perimeter. So, the focus is on controlling the actual process of crossing that perimeter. In essence, it's deciding who can access the secure space established by the system boundary." The overall concept of "access" just denotes the interaction of a subject with a given system object. In that sense, what constitutes a proper subject can be very broad. The issue can be a person OR a process. It can either be a computer process or an organizational one if it is the latter.

Lucy said, "So what are we talking about that's different from accessing data?" The Doc said, "It's more about privilege assignment, Lucy. Access privileges are assigned based on a predefined set of criteria programmed and maintained by the system staff. These criteria can be <u>temporal</u>, <u>transactional,</u> or even custom-defined." Lucy said warningly, "Terminology Doc."

The Doc laughed and said, "Thanks, Lucy. In simple terms, access is regulated by three things, the time the request is made. For instance, you can't enter a business when it's closed. That also applies to access requests to the system. For instance, worker access might be limited to only the employee's time at work. The type of transaction can also control access. For instance, people can only access system resources that they have been expressly permitted to see. That is called 'least privilege.' Or they can be granted access based on a custom set of criteria that the system's overseers have defined. For instance, an employee investigating something specific might be given access to a particular file and nothing else." Lucy said, "So access is granted based on timing, role, and privilege." The Doc said, "Brilliant Lucy! I couldn't have said it better." She muttered under her breath, "You should have."

The Doc was in full lecture mode now, as he added, "Every attempt to access the system must be evaluated and acted on based on the security policies that we just discussed. Access privileges are defined and assigned in advance based on those policies, and the criteria for administering them are embedded in the access control system. Those pre-programmed criteria are then enforced based on whatever privileges were assigned. Then, the access is either granted or denied based on those pre-defined criteria. But the point is that this all has to be set up in advance, and it applies to everybody who might use the system."

Lucy and Tom were intrigued. So the Doc went on with, "Access control embodies four essential functions: *Identification* – which asserts the user's identity, *Authentication* – which verifies that the user is who they claim to be, *Authorization* – defines what the user is allowed to access, and *Accountability* – tracks what the user did and when it was done."

Tom said, "So, we need to make identification first. What exactly is that?" The Doc said, "Identification bases all access privileges on the known properties of an individual. When you know the person seeking access to the system, you can assign their rights and track their activities, making them responsible for their actions. The practical outcome of identification is accountability."

Lucy said. "Okay, that's clear. But you have to have a vetting process before assigning access rights. So the first step in the process must be to ensure that whoever wants access has the right to have it." The Doc said, "The term for that is 'authentication.' Authentication is a formal step that the system takes to confirm the pre-approved identity of a person. Authentication verifies that the subject is who they claim to be and has a right of access. Three generic tokens are used to do that: *something you know, something you have,* or *something you are.*"

Tom said, "For example. A password is something that you know, right? And a debit card is something that you have. So, you can withdraw money from an ATM using those two things. They call that two-factor authentication." The Doc said, "That's right, Tom. But you can always forget a password or lose a credit card, and now the technology has advanced to a point where the third basis applies, something you are. So, your physiology is an even more secure way to authenticate yourself to the system."

Tom said, "That's biometrics, right? It uses fingerprints, handprints, or iris scans to determine who you are and who you claim to be. That's a pretty foolproof method since the only way the authentication could be fooled would be if somebody else was using your hand." Lucy said, "Eww, that's gross!!" The Doc laughed.

Lucy added, "That leaves authorization and accountability. In practice, authorization assigns the pre-determined access privileges that a subject owns. It's the point where the organization decides what resources a person has the right to access."

Lucy shrugged her shoulders and said, "Authentication, authorization… specifically, what's the difference." The Doc laughed again and said, "Good point Lucy. Even though they sound alike, authorization is a completely different concept from authentication. Authentication simply establishes the right of the subject to cross the system boundary, whereas authorization provides a nuanced level of 'permission,' or 'privilege' for the person seeking access." The Doc added, "Privileges are based on the individual's proven level of 'trust.' Untrusted or unknown entities cannot gain access. That's just common sense. However, the more provably trustworthy the individual is, the more access can be granted."

Tom said, "So then, what's accountability?" The Doc said, "From a system management standpoint, authorization grants each individual's rights of access. It's monitored and enforced by auditing the system logs. Then, if that identity wanders out of bounds, or is found to be abusing their privileges, they can have their rights revoked. That's *accountability*, which is typically based on an audit. Audit monitors system activities. A lot of useful system data is kept in logs that describe its computational, network, application, and user activities. These are called audit trails. Monitoring and audit trail alerts the staff to suspicious activity. It also provides details for the forensics process."

Lucy said, "So, system access is a process, right? We can teach kids about it by simply having the students set up a model identification, authentication, and authorization function, for example, for access to parts of the classroom or a school event. We could then grant an imaginary set of credentials based on a 'let's pretend' level of trustworthiness and then establish a systematic set of steps to control the subsequent access based on those credentials. It would be fun."

## EXERCISE

### I HAVE A SECRET

A popular form of system authentication called biometrics requires access to a system based on "something you are" criteria. One specific form is cognitive biometrics, which requires users to authenticate themselves based on a life event. You have been asked to create an authentication scheme based on cognitive biometrics. Make a list of ten life events (e.g., Where did you attend middle school? Or What was the first concert you attended?) that you feel would be the most secure and chosen by a user for access to a system. Be prepared to defend why the ten you picked would be the most secure.

Topic Four: Defending Your System

Tom seemed a little intimidated by the next topic as he said, "So the next topic is System Control. There are a lot of areas in that, and some of them look pretty vague. What do you see system control being about, Doc?" The Doc thought and said, "System control is a desired state, not a specific set of steps. It denotes that the appropriate set of security behaviors are in place to ensure the security and integrity of the system. The topics in that area are all aspects of the process. But we should concentrate on only those features of system control that are appropriate to the high school level. That includes everything from access control down to security hygiene."

Lucy said skeptically, "Yeah, but the titles of these areas all look kind of nebulous to me. My students need to know how to do things, not think about them. These topics might be relevant in college, but we need to have substance at the secondary level." The Doc looked sympathetic as he said, "I agree, but we have to know the standard parts of a problem to create the right solution. Taken together, the categories in this area cover the spectrum of what you would need to think about to build an effective system defense process. In essence, the topics here are the common elements of the system control process."

Lucy said, "Okay, it says here that those elements are access control, intrusion detection, and forensics. How do those fit into what you just said?" The Doc said, "Excellent summary, Lucy. *Access control* is the substantive process that safeguards the system against unauthorized access. That's the front-end. Then *intrusion detection* monitors processing during the time that the system is in use. In that respect, intrusion detection serves as the system's police force. Finally, there's *Forensics*, which only applies after the fact. Unfortunately, that's usually after you've been breached. Forensics analyzes evidence obtained from an attack to understand and characterize what happened, and how it can be prevented in the future."

Lucy, who was the unofficial taskmaster. So, she said, "Access control is first." Tom was drinking his coffee and not paying much attention to what they were saying. He sounded puzzled, "Didn't we just talk about access control in the last section? Why does that topic keep popping up?" The Doc chuckled and said, "Access control is the necessary condition for securing anything. So, in some respects, what we call 'cybersecurity' is nothing more than the various methods that we use to control access. Consequently, that concept comes up whenever we talk about security." Both Tom and Lucy looked confused. So the Doc added clarification, "But what we are talking about here is the *approach* to access control. In the holistic universe, that tactic can include everything from ensuring physical access down to how you control who can have access to an electronic file, or even operate a hardware device."

Tom said, "Okay – I get that. But, you are saying that this kind of access control comprises all of the real-world, operational things you do to ensure that the system boundary is secure. So, how is that different from intrusion detection? We studied intrusion detection in the business school, and I don't see how controlling access is different from responding to attempts to intrude?"

The Doc said, "Very perceptive point, Tom. In effect, intrusion detection and access control are two sides of the same coin. The key difference lies in the term 'intrusion.' Intrusion detection deals with any *successful* attempt to gain unauthorized access. So if the access control system fails, there has to be a backup to ensure that an intruder is identified and taken care of. That's not the same as access control which happens on the perimeter. Intrusion detection is an ongoing system process to identify and isolate attacks at any time and place within the system itself. It's a form of preventive security. There are two types of intrusion detection, *active*, which detects electronic intrusions by analyzing the real-time behavior of processing and network traffic, and *passive*, which audits the system logs to identify unauthorized intrusions. Of course, that is after the fact, but it is more likely to ferret out any mischief. In both cases, the purpose is to spot unauthorized accesses as close to the event as possible and deal with them preplanned."

Lucy said, "The rest of this section is a laundry list of topics that don't make much sense." Then, finally, the Doc launched and said, "All-in-all, what you see in this is the spectrum of things that the system designer needs to think about to ensure control. So, *malware*, which is the term for malicious code, and *vulnerabilities*, which are the inherent weaknesses in a system, are just the common hazards that must be addressed in any system control process. Whereas *penetration testing* is the standard way of testing system security."

Lucy said, "Okay, so let's tackle *malware* first. What does that slippery term mean?" Tom, who was ever the nerd, said, "The term 'malware' refers to any form of surreptitiously inserted code that is put in a system to cause mischief. There's an infinite variety of malware out there. So we can't be any more specific than that."

The Doc nodded in agreement and added, "Malware objects are pervasive in cyberspace, and there are too many of them to be able to elaborate on any further, at least at the secondary education level. However, it should be noted that all commercial malware products aim to prevent malware from being induced onto a target computer. Generally speaking, the term malware refers to six things, virus, worm, Trojan Horse, spyware, ransomware, or adware. So, the students should at least know what those categories are. They should also know that most malicious code checkers identify malware based on a database of known patterns, and we add to that list as we identify new things. There are currently over 150,000 different examples in the database."

Tom said, "So what about vulnerabilities? How does that fit?" The Doc said, "Malware is a specific form of attack; it's active mischief. In contrast, vulnerabilities are problems waiting to happen. All systems have minor vulnerabilities, which are usually nothing more than programming errors, misconfigurations, or gaps in the design logic. They're only a threat if they are exploited. Therefore, there is an ongoing effort to find and fix vulnerabilities before the bad actors discover and exploit them."

Lucy said, "Okay, I understand that. Now, what about penetration testing? I know both of those words. But I don't quite understand the process." The Doc said sympathetically, "Most people don't. Penetration testing, popularly called ethical hacking, directly evaluates the system's security status by attacking it. The term penetration testing simply describes any attack undertaken to identify and exploit security vulnerabilities. So, penetration tests are simulated attacks on the system at the owner's request. Those attacks must employ the same methods or techniques as the adversary to be effective. But to be ethical, penetration testing also must use clearly defined methodologies and have clear-cut goals. It is also customarily aimed at just those security conditions that are the most common targets of intruders."

Looking at the list of topics, Lucy said, "The last part of this section attacks. I get the point – system control requires that you defend against attacks. But aren't there an impossible number of those things happening out there? I think I read somewhere that an attack happens every thirty-nine seconds. So how do we teach students about attacks if they're so frequent?" The Doc said, "That's an excellent point, Lucy. But most of those millions of attacks can be classified into one of six generic categories, and we can teach students what those categories are." Lucy said, "Okay, Doc, what are the categories?"

The Doc said all but special attacks are *backdoors*, which are any covert way of bypassing standard authentication or security controls. They occur for several reasons, but most of them center on the intentional insertion of a backdoor during coding or because of the poor configuration of the system during operation. Tom said, "Okay, I can see that." The Doc added, "Then there's *spoofing* which describes a situation where a person or program successfully convinces the target that they are an authorized user. This is normally accomplished by falsifying credentials. There's also *tampering*, which deliberately destroys or manipulates a system. This is often done through malicious code. *Privilege escalation* is a more sophisticated form of attack. Privilege escalation is an issue that's raised in both the human and organizational security knowledge areas because it is more of a management problem than an active attack. Then there are simple *phishing* attempts that fool their victims by getting them to respond to messages that they believe have been sent by a trusted party. Finally, there is *social engineering*, which is the most dangerous type of attack in many respects. Social engineering is any type of con-game that exploits the system's people. Thus it is difficult to foresee and prevent."

Tom said, "So let me get this straight. The only thing that you are suggesting for this topic is to introduce students to each of these types of attacks and get them to understand the consequences." The Doc said, "That's about all you can do. But an informed user is less likely to be fooled by phishing or spoofing attack."

Lucy said, "Well, we can't do much about backdoors, spoofing, or tampering, since those are mainly electronic exploits, and privilege escalation sounds like an organizational problem. I'm sure that's something that will be covered in college-level courses. But I suppose we could set up a little competition to illustrate phishing and social engineering. We could tell each class member to try to get something from their classmates that they have been told they can't divulge, like their birthdate. The winner would be the one who collects the most birthdates through any confidence trick they can think of. That might not exactly duplicate a social engineering exploit. But it would illustrate the process."

The Doc nodded vigorously and said, "That's brilliant, Lucy!! The whole point is to get them to think about the security implications when working online. I might add that many backdoors get inserted by social engineering exploits, and phishing is just spoofing at the human-to-human level."

Tom said, "Okay then – the last topic is system resilience. I can see that's a noble goal. But what does it have to do with systems?" The Doc said, "I agree that the word resilience doesn't tell you much. But in effect, all of the topics in this area lead to system *resilience*. I know it's a pretty vague concept. But resilience is all the things you do to ensure the long-term viability of your system and its data. In that respect, resilience summarizes the entire point of this section. Resilient systems can't be easily exploited or harmed because they are properly engineered. All access control and intrusion detection processes are effective, and there are continuity and recovery plans in place to deal with every conceivable disaster under every likely scenario." Lucy said, "So in simple terms, all resilience means is that you thought about every one of the topics this section suggests, as well as made sure your data was backed up." The Doc laughed and said, "Right to the point as usual, Lucy."

## EXERCISE

### ATTACK EXPERIENCES

Based on your personal experience or those of someone you know, write a summary statement regarding a computer attack that occurred. When did it happen? What type of attack was it? What type of damage did the attack do? Also, list why you think the attack was successful and what you might have done to prevent it.

## Topic Five: Retiring an Old System Securely

Lucy said humbly, "I like to keep things simple. You have to do that with junior high school kids." Then she added, "The next section deals with retirement and decommissioning. We can probably skip that one, right? None of my kids will be involved in that kind of activity." The Doc said, "Not so fast, Lucy. You are correct in one respect. The actual process of retirement and decommissioning is a high-level management function that only applies to an organization. But of course, retirement doesn't happen in a vacuum. Systems are complex. And any change to the overall system architecture may affect the security of other systems. Consequently, there have to be detailed plans for retiring any organization's system.

But in the case of decommissioning – it is still important to plan how to transport anything that needs to be preserved over to your new system. That is especially true in the case of data. If you simply throw out your old computer without effectively wiping its contents, you also risk handing your precious information over to the next person who picks up your old machine."

Lucy said, "Oh Lordy… I hadn't thought of that!!" Tom said, "But that would be easy to illustrate. The kids all have cell phones, even at your level Lucy. So, we could give them an exercise where they have to plan how they would ensure that the data on those phones could be transferred to a new one that they just bought and ensure that nobody would be able to access the information that they had on their old one."

Lucy said, "That's a great idea, Tom. But won't they just tell us they would secure the old phone by throwing it in the creek?" The Doc laughed and said, "Elegant solution Lucy. You have to point out that it is possible to forensically analyze digital information even if the processor has been dunked because most of the data is still lying around in places like the cloud." Lucy said, "That is a fascinating exercise. We could have each student create a plan to transport their old data and applications to a new phone and then wipe the old one before they donate it to Goodwill."

## Topic Six: System Testing

Tom said, "System testing looks like another complex item. I can see why testing is an important part of system security. You have to keep monitoring your status to ensure that you have protection.

But the topics here seem to be aimed at the components of the system rather than assuring that it's working properly." The Doc said, "That's right Tom. We are looking at the acceptance stage rather than the operational stage of the process. This means these topics aim to ensure that the system embodies all of the security that it needs. In essence, all the requirements we talked about in the other sections of this area. So, this kind of testing aims to confirm that the system has, and will continue to maintain, all of the elements necessary to ensure its long-term security. Thus, the testing process ensures that the system requirements, design, and code meet the security criteria you have set."

Tom said, "When does this happen in the life cycle?" The Doc said, "This normally occurs at the acceptance stage. That is when you take possession of what you just bought. The rest of the topics in this area apply to the long-term sustainment of the security properties once you have the system in your possession. That's normally the rest of the useful life cycle. Ultimately, all system testing is based on the general criteria of traceability, external and internal consistency, appropriateness of the methodology and standards employed, and feasibility of both operation and the security features."

Lucy said, "That sounds like something that's part of the software engineering process. You study that at the college level, not in secondary school, right?" The Doc said, "I agree. Of course, testing is integral to the development and sustainment of systems. But that is more of a professional concern than it is general knowledge. At most, your students would have to be aware that a process exists and what the elements are." Lucy said, "What are those, Doc?"

The Doc said, "Basically, it's the ability to decide whether the system meets the security requirements you originally set for it. The idea is to validate that you got what you paid for. That analysis involves methods and practices too arcane for the high school level. But students need to know that it is important to evaluate their purchases to ensure that they have the features they are supposed to have." Tom laughed and said, "That sounds like common sense to me. But I suppose you have to make a clear point about it or some of the students will miss it. What else is there?"

The Doc said, "Well, the CSEC also mentions the need to validate the system components." Tom said, "That's way over our students' heads, and why would anybody do that?" The Doc said, "In the professional world, the system always has to be proven correct. This is a rigorous analysis process, in the sense that the functioning of each of the system components must be fully tested and documented as correct. But of course, that approach and its methods is something that you teach at the upper levels of a college program, not in high school." Lucy said, relieved, "Thank goodness for that. I couldn't imagine how I could teach eighth graders about component tests, and didn't we cover that in the last section anyhow?"

The Doc said approvingly, "Good eye Lucy. Systems are made up of components, and all of the topics in the CSEC are mutually supporting. So the elements of each knowledge area will pop up in other places where appropriate, which brings us to another topic that has been covered in other areas, particularly software security. That is the topic of the unit versus system testing."

Tom said, "Why is that important?" The Doc said, "The reason these two areas are important is that they typically validate the system requirements and are relevant to the system security area. However, since the methods and practices for doing that are more appropriate for later in the education process, the only thing you might do here is explain how unit and system tests apply to security requirements verification. The CSEC also mentions formal methods for requirements verification, but mathematical proofs of correctness belong in grad school, not high school."

Tom said, "Specifically then, what do we teach them?" Lucy said, "It's probably sufficient to do exactly what the Doc says. For example, we could discuss how the security features you want your system to have should be verified and monitored over time. We can do that on a timeline that starts from the intention to buy something. For example, we could have the students define some security requirements for a new cell phone and then put together a process for ensuring that their purchase gave them what they said they wanted to get. That could be nothing more sophisticated than having the kids confirm the presence of the feature by trying out the product. The students could even schedule a schedule for when they will periodically test to ensure that the things they wanted are still working properly." The Doc said admiringly, "That's excellent, Lucy. In straightforward terms, that is exactly what this section of the CSEC is all about."

## EXERCISE

## THE DREAM COMPUTER

Go online to the website computer manufacturer or electronics store of your choice. Imagine that you are picking out your "Dream Computer." Once you have selected, write down or print the computer's specifications. Next, develop a plan for how you would test the computer to ensure that all of the requirements listed on the specification are installed and securely functional. Your plan should include each required component, multiple ways a test will be performed to verify the component's operability, record for each test success or failure, and how you would follow up on tests that failed.

### Topic Seven: Common System Architectures

Tom said, "Last but not least, we have Common system architectures. What in the world should we do about THAT – if anything?" The Doc said, "Probably not much. That category is kind of required for a body of knowledge. The variability of system types is why having such categories is useful. Being able to factor systems into common categories makes it easier for people to talk about them. For example, the CSEC lists seven common architectural types, which we might simply mention to our students. The objective here is to make the students literate about the cybersecurity process rather than ensure they learn everything they need to know about cybersecurity. But these categories span the gamut of system types, and it is useful to know the difference."

Lucy said, "Okay, Doc, let us have it!! What are those types?" The Doc laughed and said, "Well, first, there are the *general-purpose* systems. We've already discussed those. The common architectural principles for general-purpose systems haven't changed much since the 1950s. Then there are *virtual machines*. A virtual machine is a programmed entity that emulates the behavior of other technologies. Or in simple terms, virtual machines mimic real-world systems actions using software, but they don't exist. There are also the single-purpose *Industrial control systems* that we talked about before. They have become essential in the discussion about cybersecurity because the national infrastructure rests on them. Even wilder is the *Internet of Things*, the wide range of interconnected devices like TV sets and doorbells that have created an unimaginable world of intelligent items. This is a serious concern from a security standpoint since it has expanded the potential attack surface far beyond any point that's possible to keep track of. All of these items incorporate *embedded systems*, which is just the specialized computer functionality programmed into a chip. Because embedded systems are omnipresent in modern life, there has been considerable study of best practice methods and models to ensure safety and resiliency. That body of knowledge is available for use in instructional situations. Finally, there are *mobile systems* which are not the same as the internet-of-things, in that mobile systems are data and communication oriented, rather than single function devices. Consequently, their security is a different problem. Last, of all, there are *autonomous systems*. This category is growing in importance because it involves the robotics and autonomous vehicle areas."

Lucy said, "So all we have to do is generally describe each type and tell the students how it fits in the modern world of systems, right?" The Doc said, "Excellent summary Lucy. You might also want to discuss the potential ways each system type is threatened and the consequences if they fail. But that is more like a social studies presentation than anything having to do with actual application."

## EXERCISE

### THE MYSTERY OF THE MISSING MOBILE DEVICE

If a mobile device is lost or stolen, several security features can be used to locate the device or limit the damage. Many of these can be used through apps you get from the Apple Store or Google Play. Use the internet to identify four apps, two each for iOS and Android, and create a table comparing their features. Which app would you prefer for each, iOS and Android?

Lucy said, "Wow! That was a laundry list of stuff. But I guess I see your point about literacy Doc. The students ought to at least be able to differentiate between system types since they all have their own priorities and requirements." Tom said, "I agree. We want the students to develop the appropriate practical capabilities for this learning level. But this last category is more like what we teach them in a survey of world history. They have to have a top-level concept, and this provides that. It will help them fit everything else they learn from here on out into its proper context."

The Doc said, "That's correct. We have to give the students the necessary perspective to apply the knowledge and skills they acquire later. But they will also have to understand the dynamics of radical change in this area. Those categories are like the Internet of Things, which didn't exist ten years ago. Now IoT might be one of the most critical categories of all."

As they cleaned up the empty containers and threw away the coffee cups, Lucy said, "Putting this section into teachable form might have been demanding. But at least it was the kind of thing you'd expect in a cybersecurity course. The next three items are brand new for cybersecurity since they aren't technical at all. I'm interested in seeing what we come up with for those." As he snapped off the lights, Tom said, "The next section is Human Security. It's a little bit shorter. So, maybe we'll get out of here in time for dinner tomorrow. I'm tired of living on donuts and coffee."

# 7

# HUMAN SECURITY

## Human-Centered Threats

There were thunderstorms the following morning. Lucy and Tom rushed into the building with umbrellas, while the Doc clumped in wearing a long yellow slicker that made him look like he'd just come off a commercial fishing boat. Lucy had faithfully brought the donuts. The Doc seemed to be fueled by jelly donuts. Tom had the coffee this time.

Tom said, "Human security is a bizarre category" as they were shaking out their wet things. "How do humans factor into the assurance of a large electronic milieu?" The Doc said, "People have become an increasing priority due to what's been happening in the threat environment over this decade." Tom looked puzzled, so the Doc explained, "Because most of the current record losses are directly attributable to human-centered attacks, such as insider theft or social engineering."

Lucy said, "Define that, please. What's a human-centered attack? I mean, all of the information is kept electronically." The Doc said blithely, "Information is information, Lucy." She scowled and said, "What does THAT mean?!" The Doc smiled and said, "The root of your confusion lies in the fact that the same information can exist in many different states. So, it's possible to lose it in many ways, not just electronically."

Tom said, "Okay, explain THAT, oh mysterious one." The Doc laughed and said, "Think about it; if a bad guy wants to steal your information, all he has to do is swipe the device. You lose the access, and he gains your information no matter how it was obtained."

Tom said, musing, "I hadn't thought about that. But, it's also true that it doesn't matter whether a bad guy gets your personal information from a paper file or a computer. Either way, you've lost its confidentiality. So, that raises the broader question of what is the purpose of

DOI: 10.1201/9781003187172-7

**Figure 7.1**   Lucy brought enough donuts and coffee to power the crew thru Human Security.

cybersecurity? If the field aims to secure digital information processing and storage equipment, that's one problem. But suppose the aim is to preserve the confidentiality and integrity of information itself, without caveats and restrictions. In that case, that's something else entirely."

The Doc said, "That's right, Tom. Most people view cybersecurity as a computer-based function. And frankly, protection of access to your electronic processing and storage equipment is critical. But the question remains, why go through the trouble of doing that if the thing you're trying to protect can be exploited by non-electronic means. For instance, through phishing, social engineering, or even simple theft?"

The Doc paused and said meaningfully, "So the real question here is, what should we be focused on when we think about cybersecurity? Is it the narrower concern of protecting the computing device, or is it the broader concern of preserving the value of its information that it contains?"

Lucy had been looking more-and-more upset as the discussion went on. Then, finally, she burst out, "That's obvious! The value is in the information, not the system. The computer's just a tool, a means to an end." The Doc said mildly, "Now you understand why human security is important."

Lucy noted ruefully, "WOW, I get what you're saying for a change. It DOES seem stupid to spend a fortune on a firewall and not pay any attention to vetting the guy who installs and maintains it. But I haven't read anything in the popular literature that says we need to assure the system staff. So, the human security area might be our Achilles heel."

Tom added, "In addition to protecting against insider threats, isn't the problem also motivating people to do the right thing? Most of my friends think of security as a burden." The Doc said, "That's another excellent point, Tom. In the human realm, any form of security is built around the consistent execution of a pre-designated set of tasks. The reliable performance of those tasks is essential to ensuring continuous protection. That's key because exploits happen if there are gaps in the protection scheme. But people forget, or they're in a hurry, or they just don't want to be bothered. So, one of the first conditions for establishing the human security process is to ensure that the people it affects carry out their duties in a disciplined fashion.

The problem is that humans are unique, and their behavior is personal. So, people's behavior can't be predicted like it can in the electronic universe. Furthermore, human threats can come from so many varied directions. They can be 'sophisticated' incidents, like insider thefts, spear-phishing, or social engineering scams. However, threats can also originate from such 'low-tech' reasons as simple misuse or human error. Consequently, it is almost impossible to deploy a single effective solution that will ensure against every way a human can harm an organization.

Worse, cybersecurity defenses are primarily oriented toward detecting and preventing attacks originating from outside the perimeter, not the harmful actions of a trusted insider. Still, it only takes one disgruntled worker with top-secret access to a financial or a personnel system to topple the entire house of cards for a business."

Lucy said, "That's called insider threat, right?" The Doc said, "That's correct, Lucy. Cyber threats can be classified into two categories, outsider and insider. The threats posed by outside attackers are more commonly understood. People such as hackers or cyber-criminals are the best examples of outsider threats. However, malicious actions by the trusted personnel within an organization are far too easy to carry out and very hard to prevent. These actions include fraud, misuse, theft, and human error. Because they are often random acts and the per-petrator's motivation is much less predictable. These types of threats pose a much more serious hazard than the potential actions of any outsider. Thus, it is an absolute requirement that the organization takes substantive steps to ensure consistently secure behavior by the human element."

Tom said, puzzled, "So where do you start?" Oddly enough, Lucy answered him. She said, "Well, first, you have to define a consistent set of practices that everybody has to perform consis-tently. All of our students are used to that, and they're our rules of classroom behavior." The Doc said delightedly, "Spot on, Lucy!! Those rules are embodied in the topics that comprise the Human Security knowledge area. First, there's *identification* and *authenti-cation*, commonly called identity management. Then there are *social* and *behavioral* factors, along with *social engineering* – that comprise the human attack surface. Next, there's *personal compliance* which is the enforcement topic. Then there's the need to create *awareness* and *understanding* through education, awareness, and training pro-grams. Finally, there are two aspects of privacy, *personal privacy*, which pertains to the privacy of personal information, and *usable security*, which deals with the implementation and enforcement of privacy measures."

**Topic One: Identity Management**

Lucy said, "Well then, let's get to identity management. That's the human resources side of the whole authentication and authorization thing, isn't it? We discussed the purpose of that under systems, right?" The Doc said, "That's right, Lucy.

The ability to establish personal identity and then subsequently authenticate that individual is essential since a diverse set of actors are always seeking access.

Consequently, the organization has to be able to verify the identity of every entity seeking to cross the system boundary."

Lucy said, "Entity?? What are you talking about NOW, Doc?" The Doc laughed and said, "Got me again. That means the access request can come from a human or even a running process. Likewise, the requested type of access might be virtual or even physical. But in all cases, correctly and accurately verify the entity's right to access to ensure that only the appropriate privileges are assigned. That's why the identification process falls into 'access control.' And the human security topic proposed here describes the proper way to ensure the trustworthiness of the people who are allowed access privileges."

Tom said, disgusted, "Access control again. Why are we back on this topic?" The Doc laughed and said, "Identification and authentication are far too important as concepts to be limited to a single knowledge area. Thus, access control is crosscutting throughout the entire cybersecurity body of knowledge. More importantly, identity management plays a significant role in human security.

Management's maintenance of suitable identities and subsequent authorization is the specific requirement for controlling the human element."

Tom said, "At least that's something substantive that we can teach. I accept that controlling access is the essence of security. But the topic we discuss here is the explicit means of ensuring that individual people and processes are labeled and managed, right Doc?" The Doc said, "Perfect, Tom! Identity is assigned by management, and whatever privileges have to be appropriate to each individual's role. That, of course, is based on a verified level of trust. That level of trust is decided on and assigned by management before any entity attempted to cross the system boundary."

Lucy said, "Okay, management has to decide on a level of trust for everybody who is allowed access. But how is that implemented in the real world?" The Doc said, "Well, we discussed the topic of authentication and authorization for electronic access in the last section. Now we are talking about authorizing and authenticating the humans who pass back and forth across the system boundary. As we've seen, the physical authentication perimeter might be even more critical to the organization's overall security than the electronic one. There are many ways to cross a secure perimeter in the physical world, like climbing a fence. Therefore, access control in the physical universe is typically based on human surveillance and barrier mechanisms. The secure space has to be ensured by gates, guards, and monitoring tools like TVs. Hence, physical access control is normally defined by a fixed set of checkpoints and physical devices like fences, checkpoints, and cameras."

Lucy said, "That should be easy to teach. We assign access rights to each member of the class and then break them up into teams and tell them to come up with a plan for how they will ensure that only the proper people are allowed into the authorized spaces. But it will be strictly the physical controls. If we have the right setting in school, we could even act it out by putting guards at every access point and even patrolling to make sure nobody sneaks in. We could even make it competitive. We could have most of the class do the safeguarding. But have a couple of students play the bad guy insiders and see if they can catch them." Tom said, "Perfect, Lucy!! They'll love to do that!!"

## EXERCISE

### A PLAN FOR PHYSICAL IDENTIFY MANAGEMENT

This is your first day as IT Manager of your school. As the Superintendent walked you around, he noticed that the physical security measures for the computer science wing were not adequate for the level of security he expected. So, he said that your first task is to develop a plan for identity management and physical security for that school area. First, identify the areas of the wing that have sensitive computer equipment. Then determine what groups of individuals (e.g., instructors and students) have rights to each location. Next, decide what physical security can be put into place to identify each person in their privileged area adequately. Additionally, determine what measures are not in place but should be used to prevent unauthorized access to each location.

Topic Two: Social Engineering

Lucy glowed with praise. She said, "That would lead directly into the next topic, social engineering. I have a general idea what it is but define that for me, Doc." The Doc was enjoying his fourth jelly donut.

He chewed contemplatively and said, "In simple terms, social engineering is the practice of manipulating people in a way that causes them to disclose confidential information. Social engineering is what old-time con-artists would call a 'confidence game.' But it differs from a traditional 'con' in that social engineering exploit is often just the first step in a larger and more complex attack. It's either used as a means in itself, to convince the target to give up something like a password or financial information, or to allow the attacker to install a malicious object secretly."

Tom said, "That sounds bad. How do we counter it?" The Doc said, "That isn't so easy. Social engineering exploits are pure, human-based attacks rather than electronic ones. So, automated means can't be used to detect or mitigate them. The root of social engineering lies in deception. The attacker uses manipulation to mask their true identity and motives."

Tom said, "I read somewhere that social engineering is the number one cause of loss in cyberspace. I find that hard to believe, Doc." The Doc shrugged and said, "Practically speaking, why go to all the trouble of brute forcing a user's access credentials when a simple phone call will get the same information. That's the reason why social engineering exploits are so prevalent. It's much easier to exploit human weakness than spending time and effort busting through a firewall or password cracking."

Lucy said, "How in the world do you secure THAT. Most people I know don't have the slightest idea that social engineering is a problem, let alone how to counter it." The Doc said, "You put your finger on the solution, Lucy. Your only option is to educate people about the risks and approaches. As such, every organization has to take substantive steps to ensure that its people are sufficiently well-versed in the methods and approaches of social engineering attackers."

Tom said, "Where do we start with something like that!!" The Doc said, "Well, the most important thing is to educate everybody about social engineering attacks." Lucy said, "Okay, what are those, Doc?"

The Doc said, "The primary aim of the cyber-criminal is to develop and utilize psychologically acceptable approaches to evade detection and hide their malicious activity. Up to the present day, cybersecurity attacks have been understood as a back-and-forth struggle between the organization's security team and the hacker community. However, the user community has never been seen as participants in that fight. Now thanks to social engineering, the user is not only the target of the attack, but they are also the enablers!!

As a result, the people problem is now the single point of failure in any cybersecurity protection scheme."

Lucy said, "I doubt that, Doc. Prove it!" The Doc chuckled and said, "Will you take the percentage of records lost as proof of the impact of people on the security of an organization." Lucy said, "Sure, isn't protecting against loss the whole point of cybersecurity?" The Doc said, "Okay, if that's the case, then twenty-nine percent of the record loss has been due to electronic causes over the past decade. Whereas losses due to human actions have amounted to thirty-five percent. If you factor in physical theft and loss, the total number is seventy-one percent." Lucy just sat there gobsmacked. Then she said, "Okay, then what do we do about it?"

Tom said, "That's an amazing statistic. So, what are the psychological and behavioral factors that make social engineering attacks successful?" The Doc said kindly, "Social engineering scams are successful because they take advantage of human nature. People tend to act before they think. So, they click on poisoned links or open messages from people they don't know. Then, they fall for pretexts and spyware. In short, people aren't aware of how dangerous cyberspace is."

Lucy said, "Well, social engineering is a relatively brand-new thing, isn't it?" The Doc said, "We think social engineering is a new phenomenon because it's new to cyberspace. But the truth is, people have always tried to con other people. In reality, it's no different than the confidence games that were run well before computers came into our lives. Con artists rely on people's innate trust. Social engineering exploits continue to be effective because the human mind works the way it does."

Lucy said, "That's awful, Doc. What can we as teachers do about it?" The Doc said, "If each individual is aware of the tricks and manipulation that comprise social engineering attacks and understands their psychological triggers, it's possible to mitigate those attacks." Tom said skeptically, "Like, how do they do that?" He had a low opinion of the average user.

The Doc said, "Social engineering is all about deception. The most famous social engineer of all, Kevin Mitnick, titled his book 'The Art of Deception.' Most of the strategies are based around exploiting user trust and ignorance. But misleading users is not a simple matter of running a physical con. It can also involve strictly electronic means. Thus, people need to understand the approaches used to mislead potential targets."

Lucy said, "Okay, oh-wise-one, how in the world do you do that." The Doc made a sour face and said, "There is no 'generic' way to spot a social engineering attack since they are as varied as the human imagination. That is one of the primary reasons why social engineering succeeds so often.

Consequently, mitigations are strictly limited to increasing the awareness of the user community."

Tom said, "How would you go about doing that? We're teachers. So, give us an example of what to teach." The Doc said, "Users have to know when things don't add up. The user always has to keep spoofing and pretexting exploits in mind whenever they receive or reply to a message. Thus, a suspicious user is the best approach to mitigating a social engineering attack. The best way to make them that way is through scenario-based, hands-on activities. There are several commercial tools and canned pretexts that you can use to simulate a social engineering attack. Or you can even create your own if devising con-games is something you like to do. These exercises aim to simulate the psychological influences of various types of social engineering attacks, such as targeted appeals to individual interests. You should also ensure that the student is familiar with technological mitigations such as email filtering, security blacklists, and intrusion detection systems."

Lucy said, "So let me get this straight. You suggest role-playing under various pretexts to illustrate how a social engineer would carry out a special attack, like catfishing, spear phishing, or a bait-and-switch scam, right?" The Doc said, "That's right. The whole idea is for the student to experience the attack without the consequences." Tom said, "That would be easy and fun. We could have a student act out each attack in front of the class, and then they could discuss what it targeted, how it was carried out, and maybe even how it could be improved."

## EXERCISE

### REAL OR PHISH

You can't con a con artist!! In this exercise, you will practice inspecting emails and talking about what would make an email suspicious. Begin by downloading to your computer the worksheet at https://teachingsecurity.org/wp-content/uploads/2020/01/L3-Real-or-Phish-Worksheet.pdf. Next, check the emails and then answer the questions provided for each one. After completing the worksheet, see if you can answer the following questions:

- *What did you look for?*
- *Which one was the most difficult to tell? Why?*
- *Which one was easiest to tell? Why?*
- *What do you do when you see a suspicious email or message?*
- *How confident are you in your ability to spot a phishing email?*

**Topic Three: Personal Compliance**

Lucy said, "Well, there is also common sense. Don't you think it would be easier to simply teach the students a basic set of rules to follow?" The Doc said, "That's very insightful, Lucy, since personal compliance with best practice recommendations is an important topic. Cybersecurity is like any other profession. There are a basic set of lessons that we've learned over time that address a lot of the problems that we just discussed, like never clicking on an unfamiliar link. The problem is ensuring consistent compliance with those rules. That's where codes of conduct come in."

Lucy said, "I know that that's just a term, Doc. But I can figure out why it's significant because we have a formal statement about the basic rules for proper behavior even in junior high. That's called a code of conduct. The rules captured within our code define what the group believes and how the group members should act about that belief, and they establish a general concept of right and wrong."

The Doc said emphatically, "Spot on, Lucy. It's the same thing. Every code of conduct defines a set of values and beliefs. It defines the accepted principles of the people within a given domain. Codes of conduct dictate the duties and obligations of individual group members regarding group norms. Plus, they provide a concrete statement of expected group behavior and explain the consequences of deviation from group norms. That includes a statement about the consequences of system misuse and user misbehavior."

Lucy said, "What should that statement cover?" The Doc said, "There are five specific areas where guidance about proper behavior is required. Those are an invasion of privacy, unauthorized appropriation of information, breach of confidentiality or loss of integrity, cyberbullying, and cyber hacking. Those rules of behavior have to be enforced."

Tom said, "But by whom?" The Doc said gravely, "By the organization of the course. They are the entity responsible for the behavior of their employees." Tom said, "Yeah, but how do they do that?" The Doc said, "It may sound corny. But it all hinges on motivating people to do the right thing. The willingness to comply is the only factor that ensures the proper and consistent execution of a given task, even if the performance of that task is personally inconvenient. So, people must be motivated to follow the organization's rules."

Lucy said, "Those are nice sentiments, Doc. But name one thing that will get people to do that?" The Doc said, "Of course, you're right, Lucy. That's why the motivation for proper behavior is typically reinforced by making people accountable. Those accountabilities are specified in appropriate use policies. An organization's appropriate-use policies define the proper behavior for everything from using computers to the use of expense accounts. The organization then monitors those requirements to ensure compliance. The accountability system then rewards appropriate actions and discourages inappropriate ones." Lucy said, "That's nice in concept, but specifically, how do you get people to accept it?"

The Doc said, "You put your finger on the key issue, Lucy." Lucy said, "Okay, NOW what are you talking about?" The Doc said, "Every group's responsible for ensuring that its workers know necessary to follow its rules of digital behavior and understand the consequences of non-compliance. The mechanism that is typically used to disseminate those rules is called awareness. Awareness is an informal process. If the dissemination effort is formally organized, it's called training and education. The aim of each of those modalities is to convey the group's explicit expectations about how to comply with stated policies and ethical norms and the consequences for non-compliance."

Tom said skeptically, "But best-use policies cover maybe ten percent of the predictable things. So what do you do about the unique situations, which are different by design like new social engineering exploits?" The Doc said, "That's where critical thinking comes in. When confronted with a new challenge, the individual has to be able to think through and choose the right option. That has to be a habit. People have to be always taught to consider the implications of what they are doing when asked for a response to something that they don't recognize. So in that respect, people have to develop the ingrained instinct to evaluate every new circumstance for its security consequences and then respond appropriately based on a common set of principles. That is the specific outcome of any institutionalized education process. People must be taught to deal with new situations based on existing best practice rules. It is the responsibility of education to provide that knowledge."

Tom said, "That wouldn't be too difficult. We could put the students in teams and have them list the things that might be potentially malicious in their day-to-day use of digital technology and then have them think through the potential consequences of each potentially harmful action. We could even reward the team that comes up with the longest list. Then we could have them put together an awareness program to convey what they've learned to the rest of the students in the school. It could be posters; it might even be some kind of presentation. But it would get the message across whatever it is." The Doc said delightedly, "So, in essence, you are suggesting that the students could do some of the teachings for us. That's an excellent way to learn the subject."

## EXERCISE

## COMPLYING WITH ACCEPTABLE USE

Every school or school district has some type of acceptable use policy. It may have an alternate name, such as "Technology Appropriate Use Regulations," but the content will be similar regardless. So, first, locate the policy and then read through it. Next, make a list of behaviors you have done in the last two months that would put you out of compliance with the policy. Finally, next to each behavior, identify one or two changes that you could make to bring yourself back into compliance.

### Topic Four: Awareness and Understanding

Lucy said, "We call that rote learning, Doc. It's the lowest level of knowledge in Bloom's taxonomy, which is how we scale learning experiences. Memorization of principles is the building block on which all other levels of learning rest. That level of awareness is a vast topic in that it applies to everything, but it is very limited in depth. Effective awareness programs ensure that all employees at every level in the organization understand, appreciate, and are capable of knowing and executing security practices in an organized fashion. But they are not expected to understand the nuts and bolts of why they are doing it."

Tom added, "In essence, a good awareness program will enhance each individual's motivation to practice security. The program should focus on those topics essential to the overall process to be properly targeted, though, shouldn't it, Doc?" The Doc said, "This type of teaching aims to ensure that everyone in the organization incorporates secure practices in their day-to-day work." The Doc added, "A properly structured awareness program will help people understand how to perform common cyber hygiene tasks routinely – such as secure passwords and cyberthreat mitigation tools, like virus checkers."

He took a bite of a jelly donut, savored it, and added, "You also have to provide targeted awareness programs for the needs of different levels of the organization. For instance, you would need to have a different awareness program for managers than for workers. The goal of each program is always to foster a common understanding of the security procedures for that particular role or function. But most important of all, awareness programs have to educate individuals about cyber threats. That's because naïve users can subvert any security response by simply being careless. Consequently, the overall purpose of an awareness program is to ensure a minimum level of understanding of the nature of cybersecurity threats."

Tom said excitedly, "I can see that. The presentation doesn't need to go beyond just ensuring that all employees take simple precautions to counter common threats. For example, people need to understand that Trojan Horses exist and are often forwarded to users in emails. Hence, every user needs to know that they shouldn't click on links they don't recognize." Lucy chuckled and added, "I agree with that, Tom. Once that recognition is fully established, users will think twice before they… 'Take a look at this!'"

## EXERCISE

### CONVINCE ME!

Break into teams of three and then pick a security cybersecurity topic from the following list:

- Social Engineering
- Phishing
- Protecting your Identity
- Using a Public Wi-Fi
- Malware and Antivirus Protection
- Physical Security
- Mobile Device Security
- Password Security

Next and with your topic chosen, develop a 10-minute PowerPoint presentation to convince your classmates of your subject's importance and best practices. After giving your presentation, allow your classmates to share what they liked about the production and how you may have been more convincing.

**Topic Five: Social and Behavioral Privacy**

Lucy, the unofficial scorekeeper, said, "Well, the next topic is privacy. We don't want to involve our students with anything abstract, right Doc?" The Doc said, "Well, yes, and no… at issue here is the question of how cybersecurity impacts your students' privacy rights and privacy protections. For instance, they all live on social media. But their every move online leaves cyber footprints that make them fodder for every corrupt individual from spammers to internet predators."

Lucy said, horrified, "I hadn't thought of that!" The Doc nodded and said, "Even worse, because social media sites have information like birth date and email address, identity thieves can do all kinds of harm by simply stealing and using their information. The same is true with location-based services, which reveal a kid's whereabouts to every kind of weirdo out there. So, even junior and senior high school students need to generally recognize the threat to their privacy that social media represents."

Tom said, "I understand that, Doc. But what specifically do we do about it." The Doc said, "You have to make your students aware of the common precautions that they should use to manage privacy on the various social media platforms and the online etiquette that attaches to social media use." Lucy said, "I agree with that, Doc! But unfortunately, the kids are so plugged into their social media presence that they forget that there are people other than their friends, some of whom could do them great harm. I suppose we could whip up a few horror stories about online stalking, preda- tors, or bullying and identity theft and have the students discuss the ramifications."

Tom said, "Yes, we could even have them talk about what they think the personal impacts on them would be of being staked or bul- lied. I don't know whether we could go into identity theft or inter- net predators because that might be too disturbing." Lucy said, "It depends on the situation, I suppose. It's something they have to know about. Still, the presentation of those topics would have to be handled with considerable sensitivity."

## EXERCISE

### I'M NOT TELLING!

What is your favorite social media site telling others about you? These sites have a way for you to control the information that you want others to see. The sad part is that many don't know where to go, on the site, to apply the settings or forget to go back to the settings to give their privacy a "checkup." Below is a list of popular social media sites and details of how you can protect your privacy.

*Facebook:* An excellent starting point is to do a "privacy checkup." Log into your Facebook account, click the triangle in the top right of your screen, "Privacy and Settings," then "Privacy Checkup." You are provided five privacy categories that you can click on to view and modify important information to control how it is made available. For a more detailed review of how your information is protected, click on "Settings" below the categories. Next, click "Privacy" from the menu on the left.

*Twitter:* To reach privacy settings, log into your account and click "More," then "Settings and privacy." In the new menu, you need to click on "Privacy and safety" to reach the privacy menu. The most crucial selection for Twitter is whether your account is private. If it is, only people who follow you will be allowed to see what you post. You'll have to approve each new follower, so strangers will be unable to interact with you.

*Instagram:* Log into your Instagram account, click on your profile, then on "Settings," and finally on "Privacy and Security." The main option for you to worry about is the privacy of your account. If you have a private account, people need your approval to start following you, and only approved followers can see what you post. The only other settings Instagram offers in this menu are who can see your activity status and if followers can share your stories with other people. The site also can check your account data. This is a list of all the company's data about you and your account. You can use this menu to download all your data to understand what Instagram knows about you.

*Snapchat:* This site's privacy settings can only be reached from the mobile app. Log into your app and go to your settings menu by clicking on your profile picture, then the small cogwheel in the corner. Scroll down to the "Privacy" heading to find your various privacy options. A lot of the options deal with deleting conversation and search histories. You should pay special attention to the "contact syncing" and "Permissions" sections. These features allow the app to scan your contacts for your friends on Snapchat. Under the "Privacy" heading, your final option is "My Data." This option allows you to download all the data the site has collected on you to find out how much of your personal information they're storing.

*TikTok:* To check your privacy settings, log into your account and go to your settings menu by clicking on the three dots on your profile page. Click "Privacy" to go straight to your privacy menu. Your privacy menu has several options to control most of your online privacy. For example, setting your account to private means you must approve followers before they can follow you. However, your profile will still appear in search results. Other options in the privacy menu deal with how advertisers use your information and some safety features. For example, you can disable the ability to download your videos, limit direct messages to your friends, and prevent platform-specific features such as duets.

### Topic Six: Personal Data Privacy and Security

Tom said, "Well if we decide to talk about identity theft, we should get into the issue of personal data protection." Then he turned to the Doc, puzzled, and said, "But didn't we cover that in the Data Security knowledge area?" The Doc laughed and said, "Remember the crosscutting nature of these topics. From a human security standpoint, the problem is that people simply assume that their data is always private."

Lucy said, "Well, isn't it? Suppose you provide your data to a website, for instance. In that case, they have a legal obligation to ensure that the data is used for legitimate purposes." Tom said, "But what if the website uses tracking cookies that you agree to as a condition of use, or they are careless with your personal information and lose it? What do you do then?"

The Doc said, "That's a valid point, Tom. However, that gets into liability litigation which is still in its infancy in the courts concerning an intangible product. Still, there has to be the recognition that the act of storing and maintaining personal data has legal, accuracy and security, as well as valid consent implications."

Lucy said, "Isn't that all spelled out in the end-user-license-agreement that you click on before entering the site?" The Doc laughed and said, "You would think that would be the case, wouldn't you? But the fact is that those conditions are in the eye of the beholder unless the terms are unambiguously described. So, sometimes there can be violations that lead to significant occupational, fiscal, or societal harm out of sight of trusting users."

Tom said, "Like what?" The Doc thought about it for a second and said, "The worst of these is probably personal tracking. That is so ubiquitous now that anybody active on the internet is being tracked by shadowy entities such as marketers and even some governmental entities. That is called data warehousing and data mining. Automated trackers record people's daily activity on the grid. So your name, interests, and personal details are shared back and forth without your knowledge."

A bit of an idealist, Lucy said, "That blows my mind, Doc. How could that be allowed to happen?" The Doc made a cynical chuckle and said, "They do it because they can … and since nobody in the normal universe thinks about those things, no one tries to stop them. Most of that tracking is based on electronic transactions that are an unavoidable part of daily life, including everything you buy with your credit or loyalty card to the websites you visit."

The Doc said, becoming agitated, "The power to surveil you is enhanced by using third-party cookies that the website sets on your computer. These little pieces of code are embedded in websites, and they report back to the provider whenever you've viewed a page. These cookies also gather statistics on your browsing history. This isn't limited to websites. All of the social networking services do the same thing."

Both Tom and Lucy looked aghast. Finally, Tom stuttered. "Th-that's going on right now, not in some sci-fi movie?" The Doc said, "Data mining has been going on for at least fifteen years, and it's getting more and more ubiquitous by the minute." Lucy sputtered, "That's outrageous!! What can we do about it." The Doc said, "The important point to note here is that all of this is happening without your knowing about it. It happens entirely behind the curtain without the user's knowledge or approval. That is why the personal tracking and digital footprint topic is such an important area, and it is why you need to make your students aware of what it is and its ramifications.

Then each student can decide how much of their personal life they want to put out there on the grid."

Tom said indignantly, "We need a teaching unit that explains how personal data is gathered and then analyzed and used. I suppose there is nothing illegal going on here. But, since there are no actual laws to break, it's our responsibility to at least inform the students about the risks."

### Topic Seven: Usable Security and Privacy

Lucy said, "Just like they do with their parents at that age, the students will probably ignore what we are saying because it's personally inconvenient for them. I mean, let's face it – security is a total bummer, and security measures are considered a pain in the neck by most users." Tom said, "I agree with that, Lucy!! Whether it's complex passwords or two-factor authentications, security takes extra time and imposes tedious tasks on users. So, they often dodge or even deactivate the very mechanisms that have been put there to protect them."

The Doc said, "That's a problem that has been around for almost a half-century, Tom. Saltzer and Schroeder were the first people to describe the phenomenon. They called it the 'Usability Principle.' The greater the security protocol that an organization demands, the more likely it is that the user community will develop ingenious ways of subverting it. So, the issue of usability in the design of security systems is a major concern. That is why the CSEC introduces this topic in the human security area. The challenge is that a well-designed security system must be used properly to be effective, and human beings are not cut out to do that consistently."

Tom said, "We studied that principle in the business school. It's called 'usability,' and it's an essential component of any practical cybersecurity system." The Doc said, "That's right. Tom. The political term 'think global and act local' applies in the case of cybersecurity. Most people know that cybersecurity is a global problem. But at the same time, they tend to resent the security features for their safety, like the requirement to change passwords frequently. That is because those things are the required actions that affect them directly. Thus, your students have to learn the adage about an ounce of prevention… and they have to understand that disciplined security practice is good citizenship."

Lucy said, "But what can we teach them specifically? I can't just lecture them about responsibility. They get that all the time from their parents." The Doc laughed and said, "Cybersecurity has technical and human elements. Both of those are critical aspects of the overall response. But that is a tough combination to bridge since virtual and digital, and the other is psychological and behavioral. So, students must understand that cybersecurity blends computer-based and human-centered requirements into a single unified solution to a given assurance situation. We call it holistic. But that just means that every disparate factor is factored into the response."

Tom said, "There has to be some action that unifies those various things. So what should we concentrate on here, Doc?" The Doc thought and said, "Design is perhaps the single indispensable factor since design blends all of these elements into a single practical solution." Lucy said, "That's all well and good, Doc. I can see where the process of thinking through and addressing every threat is the essential requirement for getting a complete and holistic response together. But what specifically do we concentrate on? Or maybe we just ignore this topic with junior and senior high school kids."

The Doc said, "You make a good point, Lucy. But keep in mind that design is creative, and kids at that age love to innovate. So perhaps you can talk to them about the common factors that ensure a well-thought-through design. That could include discussing making a cybersecurity solution more user-friendly, such as more usable interface designs, or perhaps new and more creative ways to automate the authentication process. At any rate, the aim would be to get them thinking about how to ensure that users follow security protocols when they are using the system."

Lucy said excitedly, "That's brilliant, Doc. I can see exactly how we could do that, even with my junior high kids. We could have them look at the current security protocols on our school computers and ask them to draw up better interfaces and suggest easier-to-operate sign-on and authentication methods. It might be something as simple as clicking on the right picture rather than remembering and entering a password. They wouldn't have to program it. They could just draw it or write it down. But they are all imaginative at that age, and I'm sure they'll come up with some very inventive things. I could even have them compete with Tom's class to develop the best ease-of-use solution. Since it's just imagination, I would stake my kids against his. Thirteen-year-olds have wild imaginations. We could even have the Principal or the system manager judge it. Maybe we could have a reward for the winners, like a certificate."

## EXERCISE

### USABILITY THROUGH SECURE BY DEFAULT

Secure by default is the practice of relieving the user from engaging in certain types of security by building measures directly into a system or software. Browse the internet looking for secure examples by default, and then write a summary of your findings. Include in your discussion how the measures you found promote greater usability.

The day was drawing close, and the Three Musketeers felt like they had plowed some new and unique ground. Tom said, "This has been one of the most interesting days, Doc." Lucy added, "I agree. When we started on this task, I thought that cybersecurity was for the geeks and nerds of the world. Today, I discover that it also involves everything that has to do with human nature. That's an enlightening perspective."

As he was putting on his raincoat, the Doc said, "The rain hasn't stopped, so we'd better run to our cars. I'll see you tomorrow." Then he stomped off across the parking lot, looking like a stork in a yellow slicker.

# 8

# ORGANIZATIONAL SECURITY

## Introduction Securing the Enterprise

The storm passed through the night; the next day was bright and sunny. The intrepid explorers met in Tom's lab because Lucy's classroom was being cleaned. Tom's room was lined with PCs, so the three of them spread all their stuff on tables. The Doc brought a jug of coffee, and Lucy had donuts.

Lucy began by saying, "Last night, I read some of the topics in the organizational security area, and it's pretty abstract stuff. I know that management's important to cybersecurity. But do you think it's relevant to high school students? I mean, as far as my kids are concerned, digital technology is more personal than it is organizational." Tom said, "I agree, Lucy. When I think of organizational security, I think of policies and standard operating procedures. I know companies use managerial concepts to guide the implementation of the other CSEC knowledge areas. But what does that have to do with high school students?"

The Doc said, "Honestly… almost nothing. However, the CSEC's organizational security knowledge area is crucial to the field overall because it is the area where the elements of security governance are presented. And having a governance framework is extremely important because it enables all of the planning and control aspects of the cybersecurity process. That's important because cybersecurity doesn't operate in a vacuum."

Lucy said, sounding slightly exasperated, "Vacuum? What in the world does that mean, oh mysterious one." The Doc chuckled and said, "The organizational security topics facilitate everyday cybersecurity work. But, as we've seen, cybersecurity involves a complete and coherent set of distinctly different activities, all rolled into a single holistic approach. Therefore, there has to be some central organizing factor that brings this diverse collection of things together. That is the

**Figure 8.1**   The crew settles down in Tom's lab to work on securing the enterprise.

role of the organizational security knowledge area. Its topics describe the roles, the organizational behaviors, and the strategic methods needed to address any potential threat, tangible or intangible, that the business might face. In short, the organizational security area packages the real-world recommendations of each of the other areas of the CSEC into a single holistic response."

Lucy said, "Explain that to me again in English, will you, Doc?" The Doc laughed and said, "All of the other areas of the CSEC represent activities that are an aspect of the solution. But the organizational security knowledge area assembles those disparate parts into a single unified approach. So in that respect, organizational security is the process that stands up the practical cybersecurity response."

Lucy said, "Okay, I understand that. The organizational security topics are more-or-less the levers you pull to construct and then fine-tune a substantive security response." The Doc said, "That's an excellent summary, Lucy. Logically, two specific conditions have to be met to make cybersecurity effective. First, the response must be complete in that a verifiably effective set of controls protects everything valuable. Second, the solution is properly implemented, so the protection can be demonstrated to be continuously operating." Tom said, "I get that, Doc. You're saying that an organization doesn't become secure by chance. That they have to do certain standard things to establish the protection."

The Doc said, "Excellent summary, Tom. Organizational security embraces nine generic topics. That's one of the reasons why it looks so complicated. But we can lump them into two large categories. The first is the big-picture management process, which identifies, assesses, and mitigates risk. Next, strategic risk **management** is just governance policy, **cybersecurity planning** which more-or-less represents the strategic thinking, and then **personnel security** which represents the policies and practices implemented to establish behavioral control. Finally, there is **business continuity, disaster recovery**, and **incident management**. That's all the concepts and practices that might be employed to preserve business value."

The Doc paused for emphasis and added, "Finally, there are the practical, day-to-day management topics. First, system **administration** involves the processes associated with ensuring the ongoing security of the system. Next, security **program management** oversees the everyday operation of the real-world security function. Then **operational security management** is the specific assurance approach that the organization uses to ensure that security protection is sustained over time. Finally, a set of practical **tools** support decision-making."

Lucy said, "That's not the order they're presented in the CSEC." The Doc said, "That's right, Lucy. As you've pointed out, this area will be hard to introduce in a secondary school setting. So, it helps to factor the topics into simpler categories to highlight their application. I'm not suggesting you go into deep explanations as the CSEC does. But your students need to understand how each topic area's concept applies to them. For instance, the first of the big-picture organizational topics is perhaps the whole point of cybersecurity: risk management. So, let's look at that."

## Topic One: Risk Management

Lucy sounded unconvinced, "Okay, I understand the intent of the words risk and management. Now explain how risk management fits into the big picture of cybersecurity and, more importantly, why should we teach it in the world." The Doc said, "Consider this… risk is a fundamental aspect of human life, right? The risk is always hovering in the background when the outcome is unknown. And the calculations we make about the result of any given action are usually part of what we do before we act. Consequently, whether risk assessment involves a decision about a major initiative, or a decision to walk across the street, we are constantly managing risk."

Tom said, "I see what you're talking about. Risk is an integral part of everybody's life, so our students need to at least understand how to assess it, even if the assessment is more along the lines of how much they will get in trouble if they decide to do something." Lucy added, "And they also need to understand that there is a rational way to manage the risks they decide to take. But what does that have to do with cybersecurity?"

The Doc said, "From a cybersecurity standpoint, organizations implement a risk management process to protect against the unauthorized use, loss, damage, disclosure, or modification of their valuable information. But the reason why risk management is a complicated task is that information is intangible, so it's hard to ensure that the protection is reliable. Therefore, the organizational environment must be assessed to identify and classify potential threats. Once threats have been identified, steps can be devised to control any adverse outcomes."

Lucy said, "And I repeat, Doc, how does any of this apply to our students?" The Doc said, "Well, a rational trade-off process is at the heart of risk management. You learn to balance the benefit of a particular action against its cost. That's called risk identification, and that is the first step in risk management. Your students are kids and do all sorts of risky things. They click on links because they're curious, put up information and opinions over-sharing, go on websites they shouldn't visit, and some of them even go over to the dark side and hack. They do all that because they have no concept of risk and consequences. Hence, you would serve them by teaching them to think intelligently about risk when they do online things. Whatever you call it, that's risk identification plain and simple."

Tom said, "I agree that we should teach our students to assess risks whenever they go out on the internet. The problem is, how do you do that? There must be some kind of best practice advice in this section of the CSEC that we can provide." The Doc laughed and said, "It's funny you should mention it, Tom, because that is practically the definition of risk analysis, which is the next topic."

Tom said sarcastically, "I thought you might say something like that." The Doc smiled at him and said, "The ideal way to approach risk is to think about it in terms of its likelihood and impact. For instance, the likelihood that one of your students would run into an online predator while surfing the web is relatively low. But the consequences of that are catastrophic. So, we tell kids always to be wary of anonymous contacts. That is the tradeoff they have to make between action and consequence, and that is something you can teach them."

Lucy was listening intently to the conversation. Then, she suddenly piped up, "The key issue here is teaching them who to trust. The internet is anonymous. So, threats are a little abstract. If a kid ran into a diamondback rattlesnake, they would run. But if they meet a friendly fellow on social media, they aren't likely to view him as a threat, even if he's more hazardous than the snake. So, it's counterintuitive to teach students that all unknown contacts are untrusted by definition. But kids must be able to assess the inherent risk of their actions on the internet."

Tom said, "That's a great point, Lucy. We need to get the message across that risk is always present when they're online. But we can't tell them not to use the internet; They'd laugh us out of school. So, what's the next step? What do we tell them?" The Doc said, "Just like everything else, we tell them to follow a process to mitigate risk." Tom said, "I suppose I can see that. But, we need to give them a standard approach to protecting themselves."

The Doc said, "That's right, Tom. Organizations adopt some systematic assessment processes in real-world practice to determine the nature of all significant threats. Your students can do the same thing by thinking about the likely consequences of their online behavior. That personal decision-making process depends on each individual's appetite for risk." Lucy said questioningly, "Appetite?" The Doc laughed, saying, "Risk appetite isn't a one-size-fits-all proposition. It's based on each individual's ability to suffer the possible consequences, which is an individual decision. Everybody has a particular affinity for risk. Some people will gamble, and others will play it safe. So, if you know the likelihood and impact of a given action, you can make intelligent choices about how much risk you are willing to take. That's precisely what risk management is all about."

Lucy said, "I can see a good way to illustrate that. We could put the students in a position where they would have to take a risk. The classic example of that is a ring toss game. We could tell them that they must toss a ring over a stake and can stand anywhere to do it. But they would get low points for doing it close to the stake and many more as they move back. The idea would be for them to think about the risk of missing the stake against the reward of standing farther back rather than close. That would make them think through risk versus reward and help them understand the tradeoff between likelihood and impact." The Doc said, "That's an excellent idea, Lucy. You just summarized all of the elements of the risk management process in a single game."

## EXERCISE

### IT'S RISKY BUSINESS

Online gaming has gained a lot of popularity over the past decade, where two or more people interact over the internet by playing a game of common interest. Sometimes, the relationships that develop through gaming can last for years. But are these games 100% safe? Take some time to think about your favorite online game and the interactions you have in playing it. Then write down your answers to the following questions:

1. *What risks may you face by playing the game and interacting with the other player(s) over the internet?*
2. *What is the likelihood that each of those risks could happen?*
3. What are the consequences of those risks happening?

Having thought through those three questions, think about each of the consequences and determine how willing you are to accept those consequences by playing the game.

Topic Two: Security Management

Lucy said, "Well, the risk is a lot easier to understand than the next topic, security management. What do those two empty words mean, Doc?" The Doc laughed and said, "I agree with you, Lucy; security management is a very tricky topic. Security management is the guidance aspect. It makes and then oversees the rules that dictate how the organization will protect itself. Those rules have to be understood and accepted by the people in the organization as a whole. Therefore, security management is enabled by a tailored set of commonly understood statements that outline the actions required and the underlying assumptions. That's security management."

Tom said, "Okay, to summarize then, the CSEC's security management topic focuses on policy-making, right Doc?" The Doc said, "That's right, Tom. Policies dictate the rules of the road for a given organization. Normally they are derived from general business purposes. However, they address all known security issues in the existing security environment and apply to everybody. Leadership is responsible for laying those rules down. But once the rules are defined, they shape cybersecurity behavior."

Lucy said, "Please tell me that we don't have to make our students get into policy setting?" The Doc laughed and said, "Of course not, Lucy. Your students will get enough of that topic in undergraduate business school. But it wouldn't hurt if they understood that every repetitive thing they do during their school day is derived from a policy. You might even make a list of all the routine administrative practices in your school, like the length of the lunch hour, and then have your students trace that back to the particular policy for lunch hours." Tom said, "I agree, if the students all understood the connection between a thing that they routinely have to do and the rationale for why they're doing it, they might be less annoyed by all of the rules they think are stupid."

Lucy laughed loudly but added, "That's right, Tom. We want the students to link compliance and the rationale for why they have to do something. For instance, the legal and ethical principle of personal privacy is why a teacher can't tell a kid what their friend's final grade was. We talk all the time about ethical principles. But we don't spend any time explaining how something like the requirement to comply with the Family Educational and Privacy Act limits our ability to post grades in common places." Tom said, "I agree with that, Lucy. There are a lot of policies that dictate how we should adhere to mandates that the district or the State hands down. But we never explain that to the kids."

Lucy said, "The problem is that our students confuse what we do to meet legal obligations with what you should do to satisfy moral principles." The Doc said, "For a change, I have to ask you what you mean by that?" Lucy snickered at the role reversal and said, "A lot of the compliance requirements at our school are dictated by law, not ethics." The Doc said, "I get it, and that's an important distinction. Because policies that shape an organization's protection scheme are usually formulated to meet external mandates, those practices might not seem to have ethical justifications. But they have a more prosaic goal: protecting the organization from legal consequences. So cyber-security practice, in general, is nothing more than things we do to meet outside requirements."

Lucy said, "Explain what you just said, Doc. I think it's important. But I don't understand how it applies." The Doc said, "A cyber-security response is, in fact, nothing more than a collection of stan-dard practices that we carry out to achieve a particular end. Those practices interact within a logical arrangement of steps to meet real-world requirements. Of course, the effectiveness of the measures in that arrangement is pretty much in the eye of the beholder. But the approach to implementing it is always the same – top-down."

Tom said, "Top-down? What's that mean, Doc?" The Doc said, "You have to coordinate the cybersecurity response to make sure that its ele-ments work effectively with each other. If you don't practice top-to-bottom management in creating that system, you will have performance discrepancies among the various elements. That's where the exploitation happens. So the solution has to be complete, what we call 'holistic,' and you can only get the entire picture if you do it top-down, not bottom-up. So, at a minimum, your students need to understand the importance of a complete solution, not a piecemeal one, and they should understand that the only way to get one of those is to view the problem holistically."

Lucy looked at Tom and said, "I don't see any need for exercises to illustrate something abstract, do you, Tom?" Tom said, "I agree, Lucy. But I think we need to spend sufficient time talking about what the Doc just said. Even though it's nothing more than common sense, it wouldn't hurt if all of our students understood that you can't solve a problem by just looking at a part of it." The Doc said, "If your students come out of this section understanding why a comprehensive solution is important, you will have given them a valuable piece of advice."

Topic Three: Cybersecurity Planning

Lucy, whose job was keeping them on task, said, "And not coincidentally, planning is the next topic. I know the concept. It's the steps you take to lay out the direction. But specifically, what are they referring to here, Doc?" The Doc said, "Planning is organized fortune telling because, by definition, the events you are addressing with the plan haven't happened yet. So, the process itself is normally scenario-based." Tom said, "Scenario? What do you mean by that?" The Doc said, "It's probably a waste of time to talk about long-term planning in the realm of technology because the pace of things makes the future hard to predict. But there is always a range of logical scenarios for the immediate future, and we can plan based on those. So, that's the type of planning we're talking about here."

Tom said, "But what does that involve?" The Doc said, "Most cybersecurity planning is based on risk and priorities. That is, plans are developed for the eventualities with the highest likelihood of occurrence and the greatest general impact. Consequently, one of the unique requirements of the planning process is the exercise of a little creativity and vision. The CSEC specifically calls out two logical ways to plan, **strategic planning**, which is the setting of the long-term direction, and **operational or tactical planning**, which constitutes the specific actions chosen to achieve a given set of strategic goals."

Lucy said, "I can see that that says strategy dictates tactics. But what's the difference in how the two are performed?" The Doc said, "Strategic planning defines the long-term path and then matches the resources to achieve that goal. In essence, the strategic planning process links the organization's overall cybersecurity goals to the overall business's technology, processes, resources, and information assets. This is typically done in one-year or three-year strategic increments. But, by necessity, it is also done by top-level decision-makers. Those people lay out the general goals under a given set of future assumptions."

Lucy said dismissively, "That's another thing that is way over our students' heads." Tom said, "Not so fast, Lucy; our students do strategic planning. It just isn't for cybersecurity. But they plan for college, even things like who they will go to the senior prom with or the car they'll buy. So, that process is also long-term and scenario-based.

But, of course, it depends on contingencies like their grades, who are socializing with who, and the kind of summer job they have. So, we need to connect the type of planning relevant to them with the idea of planning scenarios for cybersecurity."

Lucy said, "Thanks, Tom, I hadn't thought of that. It should be easy to discuss and illustrate the concept of contingency-based planning for cybersecurity because the student's plans and strategies have the same basic characteristics. It's just a matter of getting them to understand that the process they currently go through to make decisions about their prom dates is the same as what they would do if they were trying to anticipate cybersecurity challenges. Both situations require realistic plans based on what is expected to happen."

Tom said, "So, how does operational management fit this, Doc?" The Doc said, "Operational planning makes the actual decisions about accomplishing something. That's usually some short-term objective-based approach that allows the organization to meet a long-term goal."

Lucy said, "Exactly how is operational planning carried out?" The Doc said, "Operational planners specify a concrete set of actions to achieve strategic intent. So to use your excellent analogy, if one of your students wanted to attend a certain university, they would plan to do the things that would get them accepted. They would get a sterling grade point average or participate in the activities that would make them more attractive to that particular place. In that respect, then, operational planning for cybersecurity specifies the concrete steps that will be carried out to achieve the organization's strategic security purposes. Each of those planned operational steps has to be tied to a specific goal within the strategic plan, in your students' case, something like 'get into Harvard.' In addition, each of these steps must be associated with the asset it protects."

Tom said, "So it's just a matter of getting the students to understand the difference between the destination and the actual roads they would take to get there, right?" The Doc said, "Excellent, Tom; in simple terms, all you need your students to recognize is the relationship between direction and execution. The body of knowledge for planning is a critical component of most business school curricula. If your student is interested in the various strategic and operational planning methods, you can be confident that they will get plenty at that level. But for your purposes, all your students need to understand is that there is a fundamentally different relationship between the planning you do to decide on a direction and the planning you do to make the trip. They both are essential to each other. But they have a different perspective."

Tom looked at Lucy, and she nodded. Then, he said, "Well, that's another topic we can discuss, but it isn't a skill that high school students need to acquire, so let's move on to disaster planning."

### Topic Four: Business Continuity, Disaster Recovery, and Incident Management

Lucy said, "What's the justification for this next topic? I mean, it's tough for me to see why disaster planning is something that you'd want to teach? And you'd think that if a disaster's happened, you've already failed." The Doc laughed out loud. He said, "You DO cut right to the heart of things, don't you, Lucy? You're right, though; all of the other topics in this are focused on prevention. Whereas 'continuity,' as it's called in the profession, is aimed at preserving business value after the fact."

Tom piped up, "Please explain that last statement." The Doc said, "Continuity's only aim is to ensure that the effect of a disaster is minimized, no matter what its cause. The continuity process has two primary goals. So, it can be both proactive and reactive. The first aim is to prevent the complete disruption of critical services. The second is to get the information functions that HAVE been kicked offline back into operation as quickly and efficiently as possible. There are three sub-topics here, **incident response**, which is the prearranged method for responding to potentially harmful events, **disaster recovery**, which is a predetermined process for restoring operation following a harmful event, and **business continuity**, which is the deliberate process that an organization employs to ensure the survival of the business operation."

Lucy said, "Well, incident response is first. So what's that, and how do we teach it?" The Doc said, "Incident response is like establishing a fire department. It's a formally recognized function whose role is to detect and mitigate the effects of any harmful cybersecurity incident. Planning for an operation like that is both a long-term and short-term process. In the long term, the organization's incident response function seeks to anticipate harmful events and ensure that the appropriate solution has already been developed and is available for use. However, to do that, all potential risks and their likelihood have to be identified and categorized. Then the planners have to specify the precise steps that will be taken if a particular incident occurs. The firefighting analogy works in many ways here. Every fire station has the equipment and training to deal with any type of fire that might occur. The same is true with the incident response operation."

Tom said, "That would be easy to illustrate. We could have the students put together a formal plan to deal with emergencies around school, like loss of power, heat, or even natural events. They could put those in a book and then go through the protocol they specified in a 'let's pretend it's happening' scenario. Don't real incident response operations do that kind of drilling all the time?" The Doc said, "Yes, they do, Tom.' And that is an excellent example of how to communicate this."

Lucy said, "Okay, we've dealt with the firefighting; I assume that disaster recovery has to do with what you do after you put out the fire." The Doc said, "That's very good, Lucy. Disaster recovery DOES encompass the organization's actions to recover from a disaster. The goal is to minimize any loss of information and reduce the period of interruption of normal operation should a disaster occur. The types of disasters that must be planned for will vary based on the situation. So, it's contingency-based like incident response is. But there must be a clear recovery plan for each conceivable eventuality, including assigned roles, timing, and reporting." Tom had an eureka moment. He said, "We could just tack recovery planning on to the incident scenarios!! It would add a new dimension to the exercise." Lucy noted approvingly, "That's a great idea, Tom and the kids will love doing that. I can see that kind of scenario-based planning as a major unit in the new cybersecurity course."

Puzzled, Tom said, "If you have the fire fighting and recovery functions nailed down, then why do you need business continuity?" The Doc said, "Good point, Tom. Since those two functions cover the waterfront, business continuity has a much more critical purpose. The other two functions are essential for protecting the organization and its assets. Whereas continuity is more like the insurance, you buy to ensure that you stay in business."

Tom said, "Insurance?" The Doc laughed and said, "In its most basic form, business continuity lays out the steps the organization plans to take to ensure that its critical priority functions are preserved under any conditions. The planning is similar to the threat identification and risk assessment process in that it is organization-wide and comprehensive. But the only purpose of business continuity is to guarantee that the things the organization absolutely can't lose are preserved at all costs. That normally involves backup sites that mirror the day-to-day operation in real-time in another location. That sort of assurance is both costly and complicated. But in the case of a total disaster, it is necessary for business survival. Business continuity requires sophisticated planning and implementation capabilities, and it is nothing that your students would want to study. But the principle of secure backup is something they could learn about."

Tom said, "That's right, Doc!! I already cover it, but we do it as part of housekeeping. So, for example, I could make them go through their online assets and mark the things they absolutely couldn't afford to lose and then arrange a backup schedule to ensure that those things were never in jeopardy." The Doc said, "That's excellent, Tom. It's exactly what the business continuity process does on a much larger scale." Lucy said, "But there are no other exercises related to that, right? The discussion and drills you discussed would cover the continuity topic at the level we want." Tom said, "I agree with Lucy."

## Topic Five: Personnel Security

Lucy said, "For Pete's sake, what in the world does personnel security mean, and why is it in this knowledge area?" The Doc said, "You remember our discussion about insider threats in human security, right? Well, personnel security is just the practical incarnation of that topic. It's the human behavioral steps you take to guarantee a minimum adherence to the organization's rules of behavior. Consequently, the first step in the process is to develop those rules. In large corporations, this might amount to a major human resources initiative. With smaller businesses, this might require nothing more than getting the necessary information to decide what the employees need to do. In every case, however, the role of the personnel security process is to ensure that employees know and follow the rules."

Lucy said, "Okay, so what does that involve? It sounds simple." The Doc said, "Yes, it looks that way. But because there are people involved, a lot of things have to happen for the process to work. Those are all pretty common sense topics, though: **security awareness, training, and education**, which makes certain that each employee knows their duties and responsibilities, and **secure hiring**, which are the standard rules that HR follows to ensure the trustworthiness of every person in the organization brings on board, **termination practices** which is a protocol to ensure that employees are securely separated from the organization, **third-party security** which are the steps you follow to ensure the reliability of every outsider who comes inside the security perimeter, **security review processes** – which are the systematic methods that are followed to determine whether the organization's people and processes are functioning at the required level of effectiveness, and finally, there are all of the legal and ethical implications of maintaining the confidentiality of human resources data."

Lucy said, disgusted, "You couldn't possibly expect us to teach any of that to high school kids." The Doc laughed and said, "Of course not, Lucy. But you should probably introduce the importance of rules of behavior and that a formal security awareness process is needed to ensure that people know what they are. Of course, most of the rest of this is something that would be in a personnel management class in an undergraduate business school. But your students will be well prepared if they understand why the organization must carefully plan for secure hiring, separation, and human resource oversight."

### Topic Six: Systems Management

Tom said, "That's all very reasonable, Doc. I introduce topics like this under the heading of – you'll need this later." The Doc said earnestly, "That's more important than you might think, Tom. Even a general introduction to the concepts and terminology is an important first step in understanding the field. So, the earlier in the educational process, the better. And by the way, that brings us to the second category of topics, which are more practical and day-to-day. The first of those routine topics is system administration." Lucy said, "Okay, what's that?" The Doc said, "System administration includes all the functions that ensure effective control over the information technology operation.

More importantly, because it provides everyday operational support to users, the system administration function provides the direct interface between the organization's users and the system itself. Therefore, as humble as it might seem, the system administration function is perhaps the most crucial process in the defense strategy."

Tom said, "Explain that, Doc. I always thought of system administration as the janitorial staff. You know what I mean; they're always around keeping an eye on things and tweaking them." The Doc laughed aloud and said, "That's not a bad analogy, but those are pretty high-paid and highly educated janitors." The Doc said, "System administrators DO carry out the routine testing and evaluation procedures required to ensure that system performance criteria are met. And of course, they ARE responsible for installing product upgrades and doing the instream maintenance of existing systems. So, they're normally around when a product needs some adjustment to its platform, code, or the associated documentation."

Tom said, "What does all of that oversight entail then, Doc?" The Doc said, "Well, seven administrative aspects fall under the general heading of system administration. First, there is **operating system administration** which oversees and controls changes that are made to an organization's system software and applications. Those changes require a lot of knowledge and skill, and they are usually a consequence of a reported problem or a request for a change or refinement. Also, the system administration function is sometimes called configuration management. On the other hand, **database administration** serves a different purpose. It assures that the organization's databases are sufficiently protected, and their integrity is monitored.

And along with protecting data at rest, there is the other side of the coin: the transmission medium. So, **network administration** is an important sub-function of system administration. The other CSEC topics are not something you would want to present to the students, but they might want to be aware of them because they are where the technology is evolving. First, there's **cloud administration**, the organization's specific policies, technologies, applications, and controls the organization uses to secure its virtualized intellectual property. Cyber-physical system administration also applies to the specialized administrative processes for automated controls systems."

Lucy said, "Why even mention those two when we aren't going to teach it?" The Doc said, "They are in the CSEC because they are topics for venues higher up the education ladder. So, you might tell the students what they can expect later on in their education, nothing more. But if you think that's bad, the last two topics are **system hardening** and **availability**." Lucy said, appalled, "What in the world is that!?" The Doc laughed aloud and said, "**System hardening** involves the steps you take to ensure that the operating system has the maximum amount of security controls baked into it. And **availability** is the planning and design work to ensure that the system can recover rapidly from all disruptive events." Tom said, "Sort of like the system administrative side of continuity, right, Doc?" The Doc smiled and nodded.

Both Tom and Lucy added almost simultaneously, "None of this stuff belongs at the secondary level, Doc." Tom said, "That's the professional level, or maybe MBA material. You would drive ninety-nine percent of our students out of the class if you tried to cover it in high school, and the final one percent would be the nerds who found it so fascinating; they wouldn't want to study anything else." The Doc chuckled and said, "I agree that this is not secondary school material. But you might want to introduce at least and explain what each area should do. I'd leave that up to your judgment, but concepts like database, network, and even cloud administration are general interest topics, and you should treat them as such."

## Topic Seven: Security Program Management

Tom said, "I think the same advice applies to the next section. Security program management is a topic for the profession, right? So, I don't see any of these subjects being something you would put in a high school cybersecurity course except maybe just to mention them." The Doc said, "Well, you two are junior and senior high school education experts. But of course, the four basic functions in this area, **project management**, **resource management**, **security metrics**, and **quality assurance**, are the keystones of a successful cybersecurity response. So, at least they should probably be introduced and explained. I'll admit they are professional concerns, not something a high school kid would care about. But all these factors are a major component of the cybersecurity universe. So, for general understanding of the field, I think your students should have a decent understanding of what they are and how they fit together." Lucy said, "Okay, Doc, what are they, again?"

The Doc said, "Project management refers to all of the knowledge, skills, and techniques that you might need to ensure that the activities of the security function meet the organization's criteria for effectiveness. Project management aims to build a coherent and fully integrated security response. But the organization as a whole needs to make the right practical decisions about what they are willing to commit to that assurance. This is important because there are never enough resources to secure every organizational asset. To make an intelligent decision, there has to be something tangible to base it on and that's where security metrics come in. Metrics are the objective measures that characterize and communicate the performance of a given element of the operation. The formal process to collect and interpret those quantitative measures is an important aspect of security management, because the capability to make decisions that are based on explicit evidence lets the organization assign accountability. Metrics are implemented through the quality assurance function. That function is the practical management arm of the security operation. It takes a great degree of oversight to ensure a consistent state of security. Quality assurance is the process that supplies the practical means. The methods it employs are usually derived from standardized best practice, which has been developed over the past thirty years."

Tom said, "But these are huge. They're entire bodies of knowledge. I know that they even provide a certificate for project management called a Project Management Professional or PMP." The Doc said, "That's right, Tom. As we said at the beginning of this discussion, these are very broad topics that don't really have a lot of relevance at the secondary level. Except it's important that your students know what each topic is and how they interrelate."

Lucy said, "That's easy enough to cover. There is a lot written about project and resource management in the popular magazines and quality assurance and metrics are other areas where there are whole journals. We could simply assign readings on those four topics and ask the students to write up some think-pieces on how they see these areas supporting cybersecurity." The Doc said approvingly, "That is an excellent idea, Lucy."

Topic Eight: Security Operations Management

Lucy said, "So what's the difference between security program management and this topic, security operations management?" The Doc said, "Good question, Lucy. Security program management oversees everything that the organization does when it comes to security. It's big picture and planning based, and the outcome is a tailored set of processes that dictate how security will be implemented and performed in that particular organization. In contrast, security program management dictates the details of how each required process will be done in a specific project. Hence, while security program management lays out the approach, security operations management oversees the multifaceted aspects of everyday project work."

Tom said, "Okay, but what's the substance here? What does the CSEC recommend that we discuss." The Doc said, "Well, all of this boils down to your approach to ensuring that each project's security activities are coherent and correct. From that standpoint, two very general topics are called out, **security convergence**, which is the growing tendency to adopt holistic approaches, and **global security operations centers**, which denotes the tendency to combine a range of security disciplines into a single organized response."

Lucy said, confused, "Those probably have some meaning to the people in the profession. But I don't see any application of those concepts in high school. I don't even understand them myself!" Tom said, "I agree. That is the sort of highfalutin conceptual stuff that might be relevant to somebody in the profession. But this is high school." The Doc chuckled and said, "Again, you might explain the need to combine a range of security activities, from electronic to physical, into a single coherent response. Then you could stress that you must embody many different perspectives and approaches to create a multifaceted response. But all of that must be designed, implemented, and overseen through a single centralized agency. It is the existence and basic responsibilities of that agency that are important. If you can get the students to recognize the critical importance of a single centralized authority, that there can only be one cook in a busy kitchen, then you have accomplished what the CSEC is trying to do here."

Topic Nine: Analytical Tools

Lucy said, "That's a fair summary, and I see exactly what you're talking about. The details of how to do program operations management are not the point. It's important to understand that it has to be done by one unified entity. That's something we can cover in lectures or even by assigning a research paper on the topic of consolidated management. But what's this final topic, analytic tools, all about?"

The Doc said admiringly, "That's an excellent summary, Lucy. This prior knowledge unit deals with the fact that a set of automated tools, techniques, and technologies are normally employed to collect and analyze data. That data, in turn, is the basis for making good management decisions about responding to cyberattacks. The most common of these tools are the ones that do network analytics. But the precise function of all of them is to identify and isolate attacks in real-time, which is a form of preventive control. There are three categories of tools here, **performance metrics**, which are the monitoring and measurement tools that are used to track a target entity's level of functioning. These are normally chosen and implemented as part of the setup of the operations management process. These measures are designed to characterize the effectiveness of the overall security program. They collect data about a discrete set of measurable behaviors. That data is then used to judge the success or failure of the particular function they are set up to monitor. The second category is **data analytics**. This function is used almost exclusively to analyze the real-time performance of computing equipment and their associated networks. They have normally programmed devices that are configured to send alerts or terminate an offending connection if a problem is detected. Properly set up, an automated analytic system will alert management to any problematic situation and administer the required response."

The Doc added, "Finally, there is **security intelligence**. This topic means exactly what it says. It's like the sort of intelligence work that everybody knows about from TV, but security intelligence focuses on collecting, analyzing, and disseminating information about the broader picture in the cyber threat space. That includes such tasks as identifying emerging threats and assessing adversary capabilities. Essentially, this topic does the information gathering and preparatory work that allows an organization to connect the dots between emerging threats and their current security situation. The general aim is to give decision-makers enough information to let them put measures in place to thwart any anticipated attack."

Tom turned to Lucy and said, "We should probably explain what these topics are and why they're important, just as the Doc has done for us here. But this is another one of the many things in this area that are really better left to be taught at a higher level in the educational process." Lucy said, "I agree. We can tell the students about metrics, analytics, and intelligence gathering since I think they are more interesting than average. But there is no need to provide anything more than general awareness of what these things are and why they're important." The Doc said, "I agree. But your students will be much better prepared to get into the details later on if you plant the seed of awareness here. As they say – forewarned is forearmed."

Lucy looked out their classroom window and said, "It looks like a nice evening. I'm going to dinner, and we can come back tomorrow and finish this project." The musketeers cleaned up the classroom, and Tom snapped off the light. It was a productive day.

# SOCIETAL SECURITY

## Security and Society

The intrepid explorers were back in Lucy's classroom at the junior high school. Societal security was the last of the CSEC knowledge areas, and they wanted to finish the project. So there were jelly donuts galore for the Doc, and Tom brought TWO jugs of coffee.

Lucy started the process with the obvious question, "What in the world does societal security mean, Doc? And why is it in a body of knowledge for cybersecurity?" The Doc popped the remains of his first jelly donut in his mouth and said, "Societal security involves legal and ethical issues associated with good citizenship in cyberspace. That's a thorny issue because cyberspace is a virtual entity."

Tom said, "Yeah – but societal issues aren't normally part of a cyber-security curriculum, are they?" The Doc said, "That's right, Tom. The inclusion of societal considerations is a breakthrough in the overall effort to define the field fully." He added, "The current understanding of what constitutes acceptable behavior in cyberspace is so subjective that it's hard to judge right from wrong. Therefore, having a concrete basis for judging illegal or unethical behavior is a critical step in establishing an effective overall cybersecurity process."

Lucy said, "I completely agree with that. However, I can see that cyberspace is an impossibly diverse place where the rules of the road are not well-defined and what's ethically correct is pretty much in the eye of the beholder, right, Doc? So practically speaking, people need a common reference point to judge how to behave. Thus, I'm assuming that the true value of the societal security area lies in the fact that it represents a substantive basis for assessing human behavior in cyberspace."

Tom said, confused, "Didn't we cover many of those things in the human security area? Is this another one of those crosscutting things?" The Doc laughed and said, "Well, society DOES involve

DOI: 10.1201/9781003187172-9

human beings, so I suppose it would be inevitable that we would be discussing their behavior here. The difference is that the societal security area presents the underlying concepts of ethics and the law as they apply in cyberspace. In contrast, the human security area talks about the effects of human behavior on the organization's security. But, of course, with something as abstract as ethics, the boundaries of what's proper must be delimited in concrete terms. And in that respect, it's important to have a mutually agreed-on and well-defined basis for deciding where those limits are."

Lucy said, "Human actions are too erratic for a fixed set of rules. So, you always need to have some kind of benchmark on which to base decisions. This is just us teaching critical thinking again, isn't it, Doc?" Tom looked like he was about to say something. So Lucy hastily added, "Of course, there are laws and even moral precepts. But human behavior is too personal to be governed by a comprehensive rulebook. That's especially true with cyberspace because the interactions themselves are always virtual and anonymous and might potentially involve every single individual on the internet.

Consequently, having an explicit understanding of what 'social responsibility' really entails is a basic condition for judging human actions in cyberspace." The Doc said, "Absolutely correct, Lucy!! The lack of common agreement about what's proper in virtual society demands an explicit set of legal, ethical, and moral guidelines to describe the boundaries of acceptable real-world behavior. That is what societal security provides."

Lucy said, "So what do we have in this knowledge area, Doc?" The Doc said, "Well, as the name implies, societal security encompasses the underlying principles of appropriate social conduct in virtual space. The societal security area aims to present the topics that define proper social behavior. That calls out a set of five large-scale constructs that shape that behavior. The list includes applicable human considerations such as what's lawful, what's ethical, and what the social policies apply to the assurance of protection in virtual space. The topics are **Cybercrime,** meaning all forms of criminal behavior, **Cyberlaw,** which encompasses the current and emerging framework of laws and regulations that govern cyberspace, and **Cyber ethics**, which are the basic principles that underlie and motivate communal behavior on the internet. **The cyber policy** is the socially responsible decision-making element. Finally, there is the continuing theme of Privacy, which in this case is focused on topics that assure the fundamental right to personal privacy in virtual space."

## Topic One: Cybercrime

Lucy said, "Okay, the first topic is cybercrime. That's certainly a societal issue. But what's the actual substance? What do we tell our students to think about?" The Doc said, "Well, first of all, it's important that they understand the extent, impact, and legal ramifications of crimes committed in virtual space." Lucy said, "What do you mean by that?" The Doc was eyeing another donut as he said, "A lot of people think of cybercrime as specific things like unauthorized intrusions, hacking, or website defacements. But people have to understand that cybercrime is big business. It's highly organized and impacts all forms of industry and government."

Tom said, sounding confused, "Organized? Like the Mafia? Exactly what kind of crimes are we talking about here, Doc?" The Doc took a bite of his next donut and said, "At its core, cybercrime is the use of a computer to perpetrate an illegal act. The mundane examples involve individual personal violations of privacy or simple breaches of corporate confidentiality. It can also include such acts as theft of information, various forms of virtual blackmail, and a variety of statutory violations."

Tom said, "I don't see how those could pose a major threat to society." The Doc said, "Those are conventional crimes, in that they have a single victim. However, transaction-based crimes also affect whole businesses, such as cyber-fraud and deception, ransomware, digital piracy, money laundering, and various types of digital counterfeiting. Cybercrime can also involve complex white-collar criminal activity such as corporate tax evasion and stock manipulation. These are typically perpetrated for financial gain."

Tom said, "Okay, I see where those would be major company issues. How about the government?" The Doc said, "Unfortunately, there are also crimes that involve wide-scale, strategic disruption, even cyber-war. Those are squarely in the federal space. It includes targeted hacking for sabotage and espionage purposes, denial of service attacks, and there are always the potential acts of cyberterrorism perpetrated either by state or non-state actors."

Lucy said, "The students would be interested in something like that. But first, we must convince them that it's relevant to their world." The Doc said, "The most relevant threat from the students' standpoint is the rapidly growing problem of identity theft, mainly of their credit cards." Then the Doc's tone shifted, and he added solemnly, "But there are also far too many new types of crimes that target kids like online predators, child pornography, cyber-stalking, and cyber-bullying. All of these fall under the general authority of law enforcement."

Tom said, "Isn't law enforcement tough in cyberspace?" The Doc said, "That's true, Tom. But we still have to develop the awareness that we need to address cybercrime because, as we said, it is extremely profitable. It is the most profitable form of crime, far exceeding the drug trade and other more conventional ways of making money illegally. That is the case because of two things. First, information is virtual. Therefore, it can be easily stolen, transported, and sold without any conventional problems associated with physical theft. Second, criminal acts in cyberspace are not constrained by proximity. Meaning you can rob a bank from the other side of the world."

Lucy said, flabbergasted, "Wow! I can see that virtual crime is a critical issue. But how do you investigate a criminal action that's virtual?" The Doc shrugged and said, "It's the same investigative process that the police use with a common crime, except the evidence is primarily digital. So the students could watch police procedural and see the same process at work." Lucy said, "Can we teach that?" Tom said, "Maybe we could pick some current event type of cybercrime, there are plenty in the newspaper, and then have the students describe how the crime was perpetrated and the subsequent investigation process."

Lucy said, "That might work. But conventional criminal investigations are based on evidence. So how do you collect evidence if the crime is virtual?" The Doc said, "Gathering evidence typically involves criminal forensics. That requires processing the crime scene." Lucy said, "How does that work, Doc?" The Doc said, "To gather evidence of a virtual crime, investigators must make a forensically correct copy of every relevant digital activity. Then they subject that evidence to the same kind of analysis they would use for physical crimes, aiming to identify a unique motive, means, and opportunity. Since the evidence could reside in any number of places in cyberspace, the collection process normally requires the use of automated tools to identify all of the locations where relevant data might exist."

Lucy said, interested, "What does it take to do that? What should we teach?" The Doc said, "Because the evidence is electronic, the person doing the forensic collection has to ensure beyond a shadow of a doubt that what was obtained is indeed a true and accurate reflection of the facts of the case. Then the deductions the investigators draw have to determine how the crime was committed and who committed it. In that respect, cybercrime investigation is no different than the deductive exploits of Sherlock Holmes."

Tom said, "That sounds like a complicated process. A successful cybercriminal investigator embodies a mix of skills. First, they have to understand how electronic data is represented and manipulated. While at the end of the spectrum, they have to have a lawyer's command of the legal process and the investigative skills of a trained detective."

**Topic Two: Cyber Law**

The Doc paused and added, "Of course, in a worldwide milieu like the internet, the first thing that law enforcement runs into are jurisdictional issues." Tom said, "Okay, explain that, Doc." The Doc said, "Most crimes are committed in one place under a single well-understood jurisdiction. Whereas a cybercrime can be perpetrated in one country by a person living in another, using equipment located in a third place. So, which location has the jurisdiction?" Tom said, "I hadn't thought about that, but it's true. It seems like the gross national product of some of the poorer countries in the world is based strictly on hacking the citizens of the richer ones. It's impossible to prosecute somebody living in a place like that."

Lucy, married to a lawyer, added, "When you talk about something as abstract as the law and legal systems, it is important to define jurisdiction. But in the virtual world, that understanding is very blurry. We have three hundred years of precedents to decide who should oversee a trial in the physical universe. But the whole legal field is floundering because of the borderlessness of virtual space. That particularly applies to individual rights."

Tom said, alarmed, "But don't people in the US have a constitutional right to privacy, at least?" Lucy laughed and said, "It's a common myth that the Fourth Amendment provides an explicit guarantee of a right to privacy. The fact is that it only guarantees individual protection against unreasonable search and seizure."

Tom said, "Okay, then smarty-pants, how do we ensure against THAT." Surprisingly, the Doc answered instead of Lucy. He said, "Social thinking is never able to keep up with the evolution of technology. So, we have to continually draw the line between legal and illegal access to personal data." Tom said, "Okay, give me an example of what you're talking about." The Doc thought for a minute and said, "For example, third-party cookies are spyware. They are placed on a system via covert means and gather data without the owner's consent. There would probably be outrage if the average person understood that many shadowy companies were tracking their Internet usage. However, that act is not against the law, and it probably never will be because cookies are too valuable to online businesses."

Lucy said, "That's right, Doc. There is no legal protection against a lot of things that would seem to be illegal. That's because the law is geared toward protecting real property, something that's tangible. It isn't set up to protect abstract things like personal privacy or intellectual property." Tom said, "Don't patent and copyright laws protect intellectual property?" Lucy said, "The legal issue revolves around the intangibility of virtual property. Real property has substance and obvious value. It can be seen and counted. Consequently, it's possible to decide its worth in a court of law. On the other hand, intellectual property is abstract, so its value is strictly in the eye of the beholder."

Tom said, "There has to be something we can do to address that." The Doc said, "Logically, the most important step in protecting intellectual property is to increase people's awareness that intangible products have tangible value. You should harp on that with your students because they steal other people's intellectual property, like music and game files. We can't stop them from doing it. But they need to understand that they are doing something illegal when they do it." Lucy added, "That's correct, Doc. Laws like the Digital Millennium Copyright Act supposedly protect against internet-based crimes like intellectual property theft. But rules like that depend on local enforcement, which rarely happens. So, we have to rely on people doing the right thing, and that's sometimes hard to trust."

Tom said, "Well, at least there are real-world laws like HIPAA that ensure that organizations protect your personal data." Lucy said, "Unfortunately, there are big holes in that assumption. As you say, highly regulated industries like health care and finance have rather robust laws. For instance, HIPAA establishes the legal obligation that holders of personally identifiable health information take reasonable steps to protect the privacy and security of that data. In that respect, it establishes civil and criminal penalties for violations. Other examples are the Payment Card Industry Data Security regulation for the credit card companies and the Family Educational Rights and Privacy Act (FERPA) for education institutions, which we discussed back in the human security area. But these are industry-specific and do not rise to enforceable level outside their particular area."

Tom said, "There must be laws that apply to hacking. That's a black-and-white criminal act." Lucy said, "You're right there, Tom. The oldest is the 1987 Computer Fraud and Abuse Act, which is not as narrow as it might seem. Naturally, it applies to computers that the government uses. But it also applies to computers located in two or more states. Since anybody using the internet fits into that category, it extends federal jurisdiction into every nook and cranny of the private sector." Lucy added, "But his discussion about cybercrime also applies here. If the hacking takes place in multiple jurisdictions, how do we enforce a penalty that applies in one jurisdiction on somebody living in a location that might be on the other side of the world?"

The Doc added, "The problem of multinational jurisdictions has to be resolved before there can be any substantive progress toward the enforcement of laws in cyberspace. That is the main issue with cyberlaw because the internet is independent of any geographic location. So, it doesn't explicitly recognize the sovereignty and territorial limitations. Consequently, there is no uniform, internationally legal, or jurisdictional code. Yet, real individuals connect to the internet and interact with others. So, if there are laws that govern that interaction, then it appears that such laws would be fundamentally different from laws that geographic nations enforce today. The question is – exactly what those will look like?"

Tom jumped like a lightbulb had gone on in his head. He said, "I know that most of this area is still pretty speculative. But our students have civics classes in high school, and maybe we could combine assignments. Perhaps we could have them put together a civics paper suggesting how we might create a legal system for the internet. They could research past philosophies about worldwide societies like Rousseau's ideas about the community of man and pull in any existing international laws. My best students could probably put together a pretty good argument about what would need to happen if we wanted to start enforcing the law in cyberspace."

### Topic Three: Cyber Ethics

Lucy said, "Whatever those conditions might be, they will have to fit comfortably within our general ethical frame of reference. Of course, law and ethics aren't the same things, you know. But many laws are made to codify what we already recognize as ethical behavior."

Tom added, "So, that's why our aim here is to help our students understand the role of ethics in cybersecurity. This isn't something that I could see us teaching as hands-on exercises as we did in the other parts of the CSEC. We should lay out the issues and then have a conversation, right, Doc?" The Doc said, "Certainly, there has to be a discussion about ethics and ethical models if you ever want to define what constitutes appropriate behavior in cyberspace. Our goal ought to be to ensure that our students have an ethical frame of reference in mind as they live their everyday lives."

Lucy said, "That's a pretty tall order, Doc. Most of my students don't think much further than whatever their parents told them was true. They will certainly not accept the ideas that an abstract discussion about ethics would develop for them." Tom said, "I agree, Lucy. But we still have to get them to talk about right and wrong in virtual space. We can't teach them certain behavior if they don't understand that improper actions have real consequences. That's true even if the topic itself might be a little abstract."

The Doc said, "That's correct, Tom. The general concept of ethical behavior is built around a commonly accepted understanding of right and wrong, whatever that might be. Society has traditionally considered that understanding to be a social contract." Lucy said, "Social contract? What in the world are you talking about?!" The Doc chuckled and said, "Having a universal set of laws might be a pipe dream. But there has to be a well-defined and commonly accepted agreement about how to conduct yourself in cyberspace if we ever hope to be able to judge what constitutes ethical behavior. We've already decided that right and wrong can't be enforced by external regulation. So, we will have to rely on giving the students their motivation to do the right thing. That is if we want them to act properly. In that respect, we have to establish some form of commonly accepted point of reference to determine what proper conduct looks like – provide them with a moral touchstone, so to speak."

Lucy said, "Illustrate that, Doc." The Doc pondered for a second and said, "Well, most people are aware of the need to comply with legal mandates. But there also has to be some basis for making appropriate choices where there isn't a clear guideline. That's the critical role of ethics." Tom said, "That's a pretty opaque statement, Doc. Explain that to me." The Doc said, "Ethical principles tell people what has to be done to comply with a moral code, as opposed to meeting a legal requirement. Moral principles become part of the legal system when turned into laws. But practically speaking, legal is different from ethical because laws have explicit enforcement mechanisms built into them, making a law easier to understand and follow.

In comparison, ethics are focused on establishing social responsibility. The ability to make proper ethical judgments is a more critical requirement than a law, particularly the case in a milieu as intangible as cyberspace. So, the rules for what constitutes everyday ethical conduct have to be clear."

Lucy said, "I completely agree with that. There are too many variables in life to know what the right behavior is in all cases. So where no clear-cut basis for judgment exists, we need to have a commonly agreed on point of reference." Tom said, "But that's the role of formal codes of conduct. We discussed that in the organizational security area."

The Doc said, "That's right, Tom. Codes of conduct represent an organization's particular ethical stance. They serve as a statement of what the group considers proper." Lucy said, "That term sort of skipped my mind when I heard it. So what exactly is a code of conduct?" The Doc said, "Codes of conduct formally specify the values and beliefs of a particular group.

Consequently, they are created by and referenced to a specific set of people and circumstances. Your school would be one of those, so you have a student code of conduct. It just documents your school's shared vision of its values and principles. In that respect, the code dictates the general basis for 'right and wrong' for students and staff. It's a statement of what is morally proper in your school."

Tom said hesitantly, "Maybe we could use our school's code of conduct to help the students connect the dots between ethical behavior and consequences. We could ask them to take one of the published requirements in the code and give us three instances where that advice applies directly to them. For instance, we could have them explain why the code says they must be polite to others. They would have to provide practical examples of how being polite improves their school experience, or how it helps them learn more effectively." Lucy said, "That's an excellent idea, Tom. We could even have them provide a general application to cyberspace etiquette like why flaming or trolling is unethical."

The Doc asked, "Do you see any need for exercises beyond that?" Lucy said, "We are teaching understanding here, Doc, not skill. So, the students need to think about and internalize the concepts. What Tom suggests should be sufficient in a basic classroom. There might be more advanced settings where ethical exercises would be appropriate. But I don't see that applying here."

**Topic Four: Cyber Policy**

Tom said, "Speaking of theoretical things, the next topic is pretty nebulous. Why is cyber-policy relevant to anything?" The Doc laughed and said, "I think most people's eyes glaze over when they hear the word policy. But from a long-term perspective, this section could be one of the more important topic areas in the entire body of knowledge since it asks students to think about the future of cyberspace."

Lucy said, "Okay, explain THAT statement. When I hear the word policy, I think of guys in expensive suits making pronouncements. How could that relate to anything we've talked about here?" The Doc chuckled and said, "Seriously, this isn't some phony conceptual exercise. The real-world form of any type of abstract concept is shaped by the policies we create. Thus, the legal and ethical frameworks we just discussed can only be implemented through concrete policies."

Lucy said, "I hadn't thought about that. I agree that most of the problems we just discussed have to be addressed by explicit policies. Without a controlling policy framework, it would be impossible to deal in any substantive way with issues of jurisdiction, enforcement, or even ethical behavior." Tom said, "Well, if that's the case, I think we should work policy into the civics lesson we're planning for the section on cybercrime. We could have the students build an enabling framework of policies that would enforce those laws and provide a basis for judging ethical behavior." Lucy gave him a scornful look, so he quickly added, "I know that nothing like that is possible in the real world. But it would give the students a little experience wrestling with the problems of diversity that policymakers face. We could even do it like the model UN exercises, having the students represent various national interests. That should illustrate some of the issues that must be overcome."

The Doc said, "That's an excellent idea, Tom, and it's not far off the existing circumstance nationally and internationally." Lucy said, "What do you mean by that, Doc?" The Doc said, "We DO have a national policy. It was codified in Title III of the E-Government Act of 2002. That law defines a policy response for protecting the economic and national security interests of the United States. But it only applies in the Federal space, not business. So, as a result, there's the government with a big and unwieldy set of policy requirements and the rest of the country with none whatsoever, except whatever they impose. So I think you can see the disconnect there."

Tom said, puzzled, "What in the world can we do about THAT? It doesn't seem like it would be hard to create a single unifying set of policies for the entire country." The Doc said, "You'd think so, wouldn't you. But a fact prevents everybody from getting on the same page. Regulation costs money." Tom completed the sentence, "And businesses don't want to spend their money on something that feels like pure overhead to them." The Doc said, "Bingo – very wise on your part Tom. So, short of getting every critical infrastructure sector into a room and somehow hammering out a policy agreement, we will continue to have a disjointed approach to cybersecurity."

Lucy said, "But we can EVEN teach about that, Doc. As we've said, it's obvious that this part of the course should be based around a big role-playing game. As Tom said, with international policy, we could have the same experience at the national level. We would give the students various critical infrastructure roles, have them research the predispositions each sector of the economy has about cybersecurity, and then tell them to hammer out a common agreement. I'll bet we'll need hockey referees to keep them away from each other's throats. But it will be an excellent learning experience. More importantly, those kids are the generation that will have to solve these problems, so we might as well get them started young."

The Doc laughed aloud and said, "That's brilliant, Lucy, and you're right. But, unfortunately, we will need to get our house in order because there is a growing number of threat actors worldwide. Even worse, our dependence on cyberspace and our unwillingness to come to grips with the threat it poses have real potential to end society as we know it. So we had better get down to educating the next generation."

Tom said, "Pump the brakes a bit, Doc. We don't want to frighten our students." The Doc said, "Yes, but we need to give them a realistic understanding of the situation." Lucy said, "What do you mean by that, Doc?" The Doc said, "US cyberspace policy reflects our fundamental commitment to freedom of speech. However, we also know that concerns about the overall digital infrastructure and its vulnerability are legitimate and pose a grave threat to our national existence. Since we are all in the same boat socially and economically, there is a growing interest in solving the problem through national and international diplomacy. That interest is promising because the internet has moved us into a new and highly dynamic, collaborative dimension that is inevitably global. Thus, a major role-playing game that illustrates the problems might be exactly what is needed to get people thinking in the right direction."

## Topic Five: Privacy

Tom said, "Privacy is the final topic in this area. That's a little repetitive, don't you think? And I'm getting tired of talking about it. So, tell me, Doc, what could this section possibly add to what's already been said?" The Doc laughed and said, "Individual privacy calls out the principle of confidentiality which is one of the primary functions of cybersecurity. So, it doesn't seem odd that we keep talking about it. But in this case, we're talking about a societal issue, not a simple matter of privacy protection."

Lucy said, "Societal issue? Explain that, Doc." The Doc said, "Fifty years ago, when green eyeshades, pencils, and ledger books were going out of style, privacy wasn't such a thorny issue. That's because businesses couldn't collect and analyze the large quantities of data it would take to invade any individual's privacy. But now, every business in the Fortune 100 has committed enormous resources to pry into every citizen's digital actions. And if gathering all of the data needed to invade your private life isn't bad enough, the mere existence of all that stored information raises another concern: that accidental loss or deliberate theft of your records exposes you to all kinds of potential threats. That makes privacy a huge societal concern, don't you think?"

Lucy and Tom sat there with their mouths hanging open. Finally, Lucy sputtered, "What you're describing sounds more like 1984 and Big Brother than anything that today's corporate America does. That couldn't possibly happen. There must be laws." The Doc said grimly, "Legal is not the same as ethical. It's a simple fact that every electronic transaction, phone call, and internet search that you make is recorded somewhere and there are no laws against keeping and using those digital transactions. In fact, we couldn't do business on the internet if we couldn't."

**Figure 9.1**  Do you know who's watching.

Tom said, "That might be true, Doc. But what does it have to do with what we're discussing here." The Doc said, "You DO understand that everybody leaves a massive digital footprint in their daily lives, right? The problem is that everybody also assumes that their personal privacy is protected by some sort of legal means – that no third party can ever acquire, use, or sell information that you have not explicitly authorized. The problem is that, as people's internet surfing habits are captured and recorded, and their consumer behavior is kept in their credit card history, that information is being used for marketing and planning purposes. So, most individuals' personal information is bought and sold on the open market like sides of beef, and 'big data' has become a monumental hidden industry."

Lucy said, sounding outraged, "Give me a specific example of that, Doc." The Doc said gently, "There are numerous instances where that invasion of personal privacy takes place. For instance, credit monitoring." Mollified, Lucy said, "That's right, I've heard about that." The Doc said, "It is possible to track and monitor every aspect of every citizen's daily life via their financial activity. So, credit monitoring agencies collect a lot more data than simple credit history. They also know your legal, marital employment, and sometimes your medical history. They even know what magazines you read."

Tom, who might have bought some magazines he didn't want his mother to know about, said outraged, "That's ridiculous. Why would we allow something like that to happen?" On the other hand, the Doc said, "Society's willingness to condone this loss of privacy can be excused mainly because the leading edge in cyberspace has progressed so far beyond the bounds of what most people can conceive of that society as a whole still doesn't understand how our current digital capabilities impact individual interests and freedoms. And as a result, society hasn't really grappled with the essential question, 'What is the proper limit to the gathering and use of personal data by institutions and organizations?'"

Lucy said, "If that's true, why haven't people complained about it? Why isn't there some type of governmental oversight?" The Doc looked at her sympathetically and said, "It might spark moral outrage if citizens knew they were being treated like livestock by the data mining industry, but the complexity of the technology hides all of that behind the proverbial curtain. Businesses making a lot of money buying and selling your information are enabled because citizens have no concept whatsoever of what is happening to them."

Tom said, "But isn't this big mysterious data accountable to somebody?" The Doc said, "Not really. But that isn't the point in our case." Lucy said, "What are you talking about then?" The Doc said, "One of the chief responsibilities of cybersecurity is to ensure that personal information that is being held in trust by these companies is safeguarded to a very high degree of assurance. Or, in simple, practical terms, that means that people must be assured that their information is kept confidential and correct and has not been accidentally or maliciously altered or destroyed."

Tom said, "That makes sense. If somebody is holding something of mine that's valuable, they should keep it secure." But, the Doc said, "The problem is that the exponential increase in cyberattacks, especially those associated with cybercrime, has created a real challenge for big data. And, since the justification for even having a field of cybersecurity is to ensure the confidentiality and integrity of that data, this aspect of societal security is intimately involved with justifying the whole profession."

Lucy said, "That sounds like a critical point. But I need an illustration." The Doc said, "Certainly … For example, most companies have access to the credit records of every person who has ever bought, sold, or done business with them. These records are likely to include legal history and projections about shopping and credit behavior. The overall implication of that degree of knowledge is that many of the traditional rights to privacy, which the average citizen just assume are safeguarded because they were protected under older ethical systems, have been eliminated by the new reality of virtual space. Even worse, those records are easy to steal."

Lucy said, "Then we must make our students aware of that. We need to lay out and discuss what reasonable expectations they should have about privacy in the virtual universe." Tom said, "Absolutely, Lucy, I don't foresee any exercises to illustrate this. But we need to have a robust discussion about the impact of big data on the personal lives of each of our students. I think they will be surprised at what we learned: their consumer behavior is being tracked, recorded, and used by shadowy organizations. It should make a perfect exclamation point to the whole discussion of societal security."

Lucy said, "I agree, Tom. This exercise has opened my eyes to a world I never even thought existed. I hope these courses can introduce the students to the world they live in because the past is behind us, and it's a brave new world now."

The Doc said, "Well, that's everything you'll need to set up a fantastic course in cybersecurity. I wish you the best of luck and if you ever need me, just put out some jelly donuts, and I'll be there." And with that, the three intrepid explorers congratulated each other on their success, snapped off the light, and walked off into their future.